NME

MUSIC QUIZ BOOK

Written by Robert Dimery

Laurence King Publishing

Contents

Introduction

In its heyday as a printed magazine, *NME* was required reading for all self-respecting music fans – both in the UK and elsewhere. It traced pop's kaleidoscopic shifts and turns meticulously, informing, entertaining and enthusing – and occasionally being rather too hipper-than-thou for its own good.

Today's music landscape would doubtless confound a reader of the newly launched *New Musical Express* in 1952. Pop's hydra heads have sprouted in myriad unpredictable ways since then. In the Fifties, most stars avoided discussing politics and social issues (or were studiously tutored in dealing out non-committal platitudes by their managers). Today, thanks to the countercultural breakthroughs of the Sixties, reggae's righteous protest, punk's accusatory sneer and socially engaged hip hop acts such as Public Enemy, those once-controversial subjects are meat and drink to the likes of Kendrick Lamar and Beyoncé. Major issues don't scare major stars.

Once, if you missed hearing a song's title on the radio, it was gone for good; now, you can always track it down, along with an avalanche of information about the artist, whenever you like, 24 hours a day. Formats have regularly morphed (and, in the case of vinyl, experienced something of a mini revival), although the industry is still struggling to come to terms with the repercussions of music becoming available online and shareable. And, thanks to illegal downloads, free.

We're at something of a watershed in pop history. There's never been so much music readily available, both ancient and cutting-edge modern, and we're consuming it in more ways than ever. But what place is there for albums in a world where fans can simply cherry-pick their favourite tunes and forget the rest? Is it simply the artists' love of the album that keeps it alive? And have we seen the last of the seismic currents that reshape pop into something strange and new? Some might say that new music is too heavily in debt to old music to be truly original: to paraphrase one of the Eighties' most endearing left-field acts, Did Pop Eat Itself? Whatever the truth, it seems like an excellent time to look back on the ground we've covered since rock'n'roll's infancy. Hence the book you're reading.

Like anything that inspires passion, pop music (for which read rock'n'roll, hip hop, grime, disco or any other genre of your choice) generates a wealth of fascinating trivia – weird coincidences, one-hit wonders, tantalizing chart facts and stats, cringeworthy quotes and tales of excessive behaviour that serve as cautionary tales (or enticing adverts). They're the froth on top of the pop cappuccino, a lighter complement to the caffeine hit of the music itself – not essential, but everything would be a tad more drab without it.

From Christmas novelties to the blackest of metal, timeless soundtracks to music's on-off relationship with the Grim Reaper, this quiz book is a celebration of pop's diversity, eccentricity and downright oddness. Within these pages, you'll find brain-teasers on some 70 years of music-making, including sections on major artists and genres, best-selling releases, highly dubious rock-star behaviour, foot-in-mouth disease and the urban legends that we dearly hope are true.

Hopefully, it'll feel like a good maze – offering easy progress one moment and head-scratching dead ends the next. So dive in! And if these 62 quizzes inspire you to broaden your own musical radar, all the better.

Robert Dimery

BEST-SELLERS

Quiz 1

The Number One Song in Heaven

Even in the era of downloads and streaming,
the cachet of having a No.1 still endures.
From one-hit wonders to seasoned chart-toppers,
these have all been king of the hill.

Answers page 214

1.　What was the UK's first No.1 song based on download sales alone?

2.　Which song was the first million-selling No.1 in Britain?
a) 'Heartbreak Hotel', by Elvis Presley
b) 'Unchained Melody', by Jimmy Young
c) 'Rock Around the Clock', by Bill Haley and His Comets

3.　What was The Police's only US No.1?

4.　Queen's 'Bohemian Rhapsody' is the only single to have reache No.1 twice at Christmas. True or false?

5.　What is the best-selling single by an *X Factor* winner?

6.　True or false? None of the following iconic artists has had a UK or US No.1 single under their own name: The Who, Bob Dylan, Led Zeppelin

7.　As of March 2019, what was Madonna's last *Billboard* Hot 100 No.1?

8.　Who is the only female artist to have scored five US No.1s from one album?

9.　Which artist spent the most weeks at No.1 on the *Billboard* Hot 100 from 2000 to 2009?
a) Usher
b) Jay-Z
c) Beyoncé

10.　Which single was the last UK No.1 of the 1970s and the first No.1 of the 1980s?

11.　Only one act has topped the UK chart in five consecutive decades. Who?

12. **Three singles share the distinction of reaching No.1 three times in the UK. What is the most recent?**
    a) 'Bohemian Rhapsody', by Queen
    b) 'Happy', by Pharrell Williams
    c) 'Imagine', by John Lennon

13. **Which No.1 was the fastest-selling single ever in the UK?**
    a) 'Evergreen', by Will Young
    b) 'She Loves You', by The Beatles
    c) 'Thinking Out Loud', by Ed Sheeran

14. **Which brooding synth-pop classic did Joe Dolce's 'Shaddap You Face' keep off the UK No.1 spot in 1982?**

15. **Rihanna's 'Umbrella' enjoyed a ten-week stay at the top of the UK charts in 2007. What single replaced it?**

16. **Name one of the two songs that share the record for most weeks at No.1 on the *Billboard* Hot 100.**

Quiz 2

One in Every Home

Reports of the album's death have been greatly exaggerated. Despite the threat posed by streaming, there's something about its format that artists just love. And what a history it's had ...

Answers page 215

1. The Clash mimicked the cover of Elvis Presley's eponymous debut LP for their 1979 magnum opus. What was it called?
   a) *The Clash*
   b) *Give 'Em Enough Rope*
   c) *London Calling*

2. A former glam-rock star scored the best-selling album in the USA in 1994 with a roaringly popular soundtrack. Name the singer and (if you can) the soundtrack.

3. Losing their charismatic lead singer didn't slow this electrifying rock band down. The first album released after his death has sold around 50 million copies, making it one of history's best-sellers. Name the LP and the band.

4. A soundtrack holds the record for the longest stay at No.1 on *Billboard*, topping the listings for 54 weeks and becoming the best-selling album in the USA in both 1962 and 1963. What was it?
   a) *West Side Story*
   b) *Fiddler on the Roof*
   c) *South Pacific*

5. Who were the first band to see their first four albums debut at No.1 on the *Billboard* 200?

6. How do you solve a problem like this? It was the UK's best-selling LP in 1965, 1966 and 1968, and wound up as the second best-selling album of the Sixties – though it might not be one of your favourite things. Name it.

7. Which British quintet had the best-selling LP in the USA in 1997?

8. What's the UK's fastest-selling album ever?
   a) *Thank U, Next* (2019), by Ariana Grande
   b) *25* (2015), by Adele
   c) *X&Y* (2005), by Coldplay

9. Which of the following *Now That's What I Call Music!* compilations failed to reach No.1 in the UK?
   a) *4*
   b) *5*
   c) *6*

10. Brian Eno was once producing both Coldplay and U2 at around the same time – and was terrified that he'd mix up the music for the two albums. Name either of the LPs he was working on.

11. REM's first US No.1 album was *Murmur* (1983). True or false?

12. 'Hand in My Pocket', 'You Learn' and 'All I Really Want' all featured on the best-selling LP of 1996. Name the album and its Canadian creator.

13. Released in 2000, this album was unconditionally the USA's best-selling LP of that year – and, indeed, of the whole of the decade. Name it.

14. Ed Sheeran had the UK's best-selling albums in 2014 and 2017. Name either of the symbolic chart-topping albums to achieve this feat.

15. All except one of Lady Gaga's albums have reached No.1 on the *Billboard* 200 chart. What is the exception?

16. Which Sixties duo scored the best-selling album of the 1970s in the UK, with their last studio LP together? And what was the crossover album?

DID YOU KNOW?
At its peak, Michael Jackson's *Thriller* album was selling a million copies every week.

Quiz 3

The Winner Takes It All

Some artists carp that awards are a pointless distraction from their music. But we're guessing lots of them secretly like the recognition. Not to mention the money. Although having said that ...

Answers page 216

1. Which infamously hedonistic band promptly lost their £20,000 cheque for winning the inaugural Mercury Music Prize in 1992?

2. When Michael Jackson assumed a Christ-like demeanour for a performance of 'Earth Song' at the 1996 BRIT Awards, another singer jumped onstage to protest. Class! Do you remember the stage invader?

3. Joris de Man's music for the video game *Killzone 2* won the first Ivor Novello music award for a gaming soundtrack. In what year?
    a) 2006
    b) 2010
    c) 2014

4. These critics' darlings have been nominated for the Mercury Prize five times and the BRIT Awards on 17 occasions – and have never won either. You must be kidding, eh? Name them.

5. As of March 2019, which rapper has the most Grammy wins, with 22?

6. Composer A.R. Rahman picked up the 2009 Academy Award for Best Original Score (and another for co-writing the Best Original Song). What was the movie in question?
    a) *A Wednesday!* (2008)
    b) *Welcome to Sajjanpur* (2008)
    c) *Slumdog Millionaire* (2008)

7. Which Sun-kissed performer won his first Grammy in 1967 for the gospel song 'How Great Thou Art'?

8. At the 1992 BRITs, which act (big breath): contrarily delivered a death-metal version of one of their biggest hits and machine-gunned blanks over the audience before dumping a dead sheep bearing the legend 'I died for you [bon appetit]' outside the after-party?

9. Who (and what) won the first Grammy for Album of the Year?
    a) Henry Mancini, for *The Music from Peter Gunn*
    b) Frank Sinatra, for *Come Fly with Me*
    c) The Original Broadway Cast, for *My Fair Lady*

10. In 2017, Beyoncé picked up two Grammys but - once again - not the coveted Best Album gong, prompting a fellow performer to complain backstage, 'What the fuck does she have to do to win Album of the Year?' Name Bey's champion.

11. What was the first Disney movie to win an Academy Award for Best Original Score?
    a) *Snow White and the Seven Dwarfs* (1937)
    b) *Pinocchio* (1940)
    c) *Dumbo* (1941)

12. Which immortal drum and bass album won Album of the Year at the first MOBO Awards?

13. Which artist has won the most MTV Video Music Awards in a single night?
    a) Madonna
    b) Peter Gabriel
    c) Green Day

14. Which drippy Burt Bacharach/Hal David song won the Academy Award for Best Original Song in 1970?

15. Which band has won the most Grammy Awards for Best Metal Performance?
    a) Metallica
    b) Nine Inch Nails
    c) Slayer

16. Which former boy-band singer has won the most BRIT Awards?

DID YOU KNOW?
The absolute record for most Grammy Awards in any genre is held by conductor Georg Solti, with 31. Tied in second place are producer Quincy Jones and country singer Alison Krauss, with 27 each.

Quiz 4

Santa Claus Is Comin' to Town

Who doesn't love a bit of cheese at Christmas –
whether it's George Michael in a chunky
knit mourning a past romance under
the mistletoe or a be-tartanned Noddy Holder
bellowing about rock'n'rolling grannies.
One more mince pie? Oh go on then ...

Answers page 217

1. She played Catwoman on US TV in the Sixties and cooed 'Santa Baby' in 1953. Who on Earth is she?

2. What monumental event occurred on (and rather overshadowed) the day Phil Spector's classic album *A Christmas Gift for You* was released?
    a) US president John F. Kennedy was shot
    b) Yuri Gagarin became the first man in outer space
    c) The Beatles arrived in the USA

3. In which Bing Crosby movie did the song 'White Christmas' first appear?
    a) *Holiday Inn* (1942)
    b) *The Bells of St. Mary's* (1945)
    c) *White Christmas* (1954)

4. Speaking of Bing, in 1982 he scored a Christmas UK No.3 hit with an unlikely duet. Who was his stellar singing partner?

5. The opening line to which Nat King Cole seasonal hit speaks of roasting chestnuts and an open fire?

6. Frankie Goes To Hollywood's 1984 festive smash 'The Power of Love' achieved a rare feat in the annals of pop. What?
    a) It stayed at No.1 for 10 weeks
    b) It sold over 5 million copies
    c) It was the third of their first three singles to reach No.1 in the UK

7. Debuting in 1934, this hit Christmas tune anticipating Father Christmas's arrival is the most played holiday song of the past 50 years. It's been covered by Bing Crosby, The Crystals, Bruce Springsteen and The Supremes among others. What is it?

8. Which member of prog-rock gods Emerson, Lake & Palmer had a melancholy festive UK No.2 in 1975 with 'I Believe in Father Christmas'?
    a) Keith Emerson
    b) Greg Lake
    c) Carl Palmer

9. **What's the most played Christmas song of the 21st century?**
a) 'White Christmas', by Bing Crosby
b) 'The Christmas Song (Merry Christmas to You)', by Nat King Cole
c) 'Fairytale of New York', by The Pogues feat. Kirsty MacColl

10. **How many times has 'Do They Know It's Christmas?' topped the UK charts?**
a) Three
b) Four
c) Five

11. **What rival festive tune kept Wizzard's 'I Wish It Could Be Christmas Everyday' off the UK No.1 spot in 1973?**

12. **Which 1971 Christmas song is subtitled '(War is Over)'?**

13. **Harry Belafonte had a hit with 'Mary's Boy Child' in 1956. Who topped the UK charts with the song during Christmas 1978?**
a) Johnny Mathis
b) Boney M
c) Andy Williams

14. **Who demanded 'Stop the Cavalry' in 1980?**

15. **In the 1990s, one band enjoyed three consecutive (non-Christmassy) Christmas No.1s in the UK. Who were they? And for an extra point, who was the only act ever to have achieved the same feat beforehand?**

16. **Mud's 1974 downbeat festive chart-topper 'Lonely This Christmas' was originally recorded by Elvis Presley. True or false?**

DID YOU KNOW?
Band Aid's 'Do They Know It's Christmas?' is the UK's best-selling Christmas No.1.

Quiz 5

Cover Me

The original may be great, but the cover is often greater. Think Dylan's 'All Along the Watchtower' by Jimi Hendrix, or The Zutons' 'Valerie' as reimagined by Mark Ronson and Amy Winehouse. So: how covered up are you?

Answers page 218

1. Who scored a transatlantic No.1 in 1965 with their version of Bob Dylan's 'Mr. Tambourine Man'?

2. Happy Mondays' biggest-selling single was a cover version. Name it, and the original artist.

3. Which Rolling Stones song was covered by Otis Redding, Aretha Franklin, Cat Power, Devo and The Residents, among others?

4. Motown founder Berry Gordy co-wrote a song that was later covered by The Beatles and The Flying Lizards, to name but two. What was it?

5. In 1979, disco starlet Amii Stewart recorded a hit version (US No.1/UK No.6) of a soul stomper first recorded by Eddie Floyd in 1966. Name it.

6. Name one artist, apart from its composer Leonard Cohen, who has recorded 'Hallelujah'.

7. Beyoncé covered it, but Whitney Houston's version of this song of eternal love – composed by Dolly Parton – remains definitive. What is it?

8. One post-punk band dropped a host of cover versions during their career, including 'Victoria' (The Kinks), 'Mr. Pharmacist' (The Other Half), 'White Lightning' (Waylon Jennings), 'There's a Ghost in My House' (R. Dean Taylor) and 'Lost in Music' (Sister Sledge). Who were they?

9. Robert Wyatt recorded a memorable cover of the song 'Shipbuilding' in 1982. Who wrote the lyrics?
   a) Nick Lowe
   b) Elvis Costello
   c) Paul Weller

10. Paul Revere and the Raiders and (more famously) The Monkees recorded garage-rock classic '(I'm Not Your) Steppin' Stone' in 1966. Which controversial UK punk band later covered it live?

11. Fugees' take on 'Killing Me Softly with His Song' picked up a Grammy in 1997. Who took it to No.1 in the USA and Canada (and No.6 in the UK) in 1973?
   a) Diana Ross
   b) Barbra Streisand
   c) Roberta Flack

12. Which 1969 Creedence Clearwater Revival tune about a Mississippi steamboat was later famously covered by Solomon Burke, Ike and Tina Turner and Elvis Presley?

13. Johnny Cash covered a painfully frank Nine Inch Nails song in 2003, inspiring its composer to admit, 'That song isn't mine anymore.' What was it?
   a) 'Head Like a Hole'
   b) 'Hurt'
   c) 'The Big Come Down'

14. What was the cryptic name of Guns N' Roses' 1993 covers-only album?
   a) *Use Your Illusion I*
   b) *Chinese Democracy*
   c) *"The Spaghetti Incident?"*

15. Which rose-tinted tune – and Edith Piaf's signature song – did Grace Jones take to No.3 in France in 1977?

16. Soft Cell took Northern Soul classic 'Tainted Love' to No.1 in the UK in 1981. The original singer had been Marc Bolan's girlfriend. Name her.

SAY WHAT?
'I had no expectations of it at all. All I thought about was singing it in tune!' Robert Wyatt on his definitive version of 'Shipbuilding' (*NME*, 4 June 1983)

Quiz 6

Once in a Lifetime

Why spend years releasing album after album? Sometimes one hit song is all it takes to make your mark in pop history ...

Answers page 219

1. **Which of the following was 'Play That Funky Music' a hit for?**
   a) The Average White Band
   b) Dr. Hook
   c) Wild Cherry

2. **The Teddy Bears' *Billboard* No.1 'To Know Him Is to Love Him' (1958) was later covered by everyone from The Beatles to Amy Winehouse. Which Teddy Bear went on to become one of the most famous producers of all time?**

3. **Whose mom were Fountains of Wayne serenading in 2003?**
   a) Macy's
   b) Tracy's
   c) Stacy's

4. **Anita Ward announced herself with which disco smash in 1979?**
   a) 'Shame, Shame, Shame'
   b) 'Call Me'
   c) 'Ring My Bell'

5. **Toni Basil was once a choreographer for The Monkees and had a hit song in 1982 that shared the name of one of them. Name it.**

6. **What piece of reassuring advice did Bobby McFerrin offer in 1988?**

7. **Which mambo number took Lou Bega into the charts in 1999?**
   a) 'Mambo No.1'
   b) 'Mambo No.5'
   c) 'Mambo No.9'

8. **What was it raining in The Weather Girls' 1982 hit single?**

9. **Who exorted us to 'Jump Around' in 1992?**
   a) House of Love
   b) House of Broken Dreams
   c) House of Pain

10. **Iron Butterfly's signature tune was 'In-A-Gadda-Da-Vida' (1968). But that was actually a misheard version of the original Bible-related title – which was ...?**

11. Who penned Sinéad O'Connor's sole international No.1 'Nothing Compares 2 U'?

12. It was the first major rap hit, in 1979, but regarded as a one-off novelty at the time. The act was The Sugarhill Gang. The tune was ...?

13. The hook for Vanilla Ice's 'Ice Ice Baby' (1990) sampled which Queen/David Bowie song?

14. What question were Baha Men asking in 2000?
    a) 'Can I Touch It?'
    b) 'So What?'
    c) 'Who Let the Dogs Out?'

15. Stateside, Snow Patrol's only major hit was 'Chasing Cars', a *Billboard* No.5 in 2006. In the UK, it was the last song to be performed on a famous British TV music programme before its cancellation. What was the show?
    a) *Later ...*
    b) *The Tube*
    c) *Top of the Pops*

16. Released in 2003, Eamon's No.1 'Fuck It (I Don't Want You Back)' prompted an answer song, which itself became a hit. What was it?

DID YOU KNOW?
Snow Patrol's 'Chasing Cars' was the most played song of the decade in the UK.

DECADE
BY DECADE

Quiz 1

The Fifties

NME was born in 1952. Jazz dominated its pages. By the end of the decade, though, it was rock'n'roll through and through.

Answers page 220

1. Which Fifties teen idol – later namechecked in a song by Dexys Midnight Runners – was known as the 'Prince of Wails' and the 'Nabob of Sob'?

2. This Country & Western icon wrote a string of standards, including 'Your Cheatin' Heart' and 'Hey, Good Lookin''. He died of heart failure in the back of a car on New Year's Eve, 1952. Name him.

3. One fiery rock'n'roller's behaviour prompted questions in the House of Commons in June 1958. Which one?

4. What was the first single to enter the UK charts at No.1?

5. The man dubbed the 'Father of the Blues' died on 28 March 1958. What was his real name?
    a) W.C. Handy
    b) B.B. King
    c) Robert Johnson

6. In The Everly Brothers' song 'Wake Up Little Susie', what time in the morning did the stay-out teens actually wake?
    a) Midnight
    b) Two o'clock
    c) Four o'clock

7. Fifties singer Pat Boone's suede shoes became one of his trademarks. What colour were they?
    a) Blue
    b) Red
    c) White

8. Name any one of the five best-selling singles in the USA during the 1950s.

9. 'At the Hop' was a 1958 *Billboard* No.1 for which act?
    a) Danny and The Juniors
    b) The Teenagers
    c) Johnny 'Man' Young

10. In the 1970s, a Sid Vicious-helmed Sex Pistols covered two Fifties rock'n'roll classics: 'Something Else' and 'C'mon Everybody'. Who wrote and recorded them originally?

11. 'The most brutal, ugly, degenerate, vicious form of expression it has been my displeasure to hear – naturally I refer to the bulk of rock'n'roll.' Which crooner penned these words in 1957?
    a) Bing Crosby
    b) Tony Bennett
    c) Frank Sinatra

12. Name one of the singers who had a major hit with 'Singing the Blues' in 1956.

13. By what name is Harry Rodger Webb better known?

14. Julie London's torch song 'Cry Me a River' appeared in an iconic rock'n'roll movie that starred Jayne Mansfield in the title role. Name it.

15. Who wrote 'Blue Suede Shoes'?
    a) Elvis Presley
    b) Little Richard
    c) Carl Perkins

16. Premiering on 26 September 1957, *West Side Story* has gone down as one of history's greatest musicals. Which Shakespeare play was it based on?

SAY WHAT?
'Official – World Record! The *NME* proudly announces the Largest Circulation in the World for any musical paper. Certified audited weekly sales guaranteed exceed ... 100,000.' (*NME*, 4 February 1955)

Quiz 2

The Sixties

Long hair, short skirts, peace, revolution,
Beatles, Stones ... Turn up, tune in and
drop into the quiz of the decade.

Answers page 221

1. What was The Rolling Stones' first US No.1 single?

2. What was the title of Elvis Presley's first post-Army album, released in 1960?
   a) *Elvis Is Back!*
   b) *Back in the USA!*
   c) *The Return of the King!*

3. Which member of The Who played French horn?

4. Dusty Springfield had a UK No.1 in 1965 with a rewrite of the Italian song 'Io che non vivo (senza te)'. By what name is it better known?

5. Name any two of the bands with which Steve Winwood charted in the 1960s.

6. How many hours away from Tulsa was Gene Pitney in the 1963 transatlantic hit song of the same name?
   a) 48
   b) 12
   c) 24

7. The best-selling album of 1965 on *Billboard* was a soundtrack from a movie starring Julie Andrews. Name it.

8. In 1968, who became the first artist to have a posthumous *Billboard* No.1?

9. On the TV show *Happening for Lulu* in 1968, The Jimi Hendrix Experience abruptly stopped playing one of their hits and started a song by Cream, who had just split up. What was the Cream song?
   a) 'Sunshine of Your Love'
   b) 'Strange Brew'
   c) 'I Feel Free'

10. Pink Floyd's 1967 debut album *The Piper at the Gates of Dawn* was named after a chapter in a classic children's book. Which one?
    a) *Alice's Adventures in Wonderland*, by Lewis Carroll (1865)
    b) *The Water-Babies*, by Charles Kingsley (1863)
    c) *The Wind in the Willows*, by Kenneth Grahame (1908)

11. During the Sixties, lyricists Tony Asher and Van Dyke Parks worked with which West Coast songwriter?

12. Name at least one of Crosby, Stills & Nash's famous original bands.

13. The Supremes were once nicknamed the 'no-hit Supremes' for their lack of chart action. What was their first US No.1?
    a) 'Baby Love'
    b) 'Where Did Our Love Go'
    c) 'Stop! In the Name of Love'

14. Her 1971 album *Tapestry* was one of the decade's best-sellers, but in the 1960s this prolific songwriter only had one hit single under her own name: 'It Might as Well Rain Until September' (1962 – a UK No.3, US No.22). Name her.

15. Gerry and the Pacemakers achieved an unprecedented chart feat in 1963. What was it?
    a) Their debut single returned to the No.1 spot three times
    b) They had a simultaneous US and UK No.1
    c) Their first three singles all reached No.1 in the UK

16. Which artist visited 'Desolation Row', 'Positively 4th Street' and 'Highway 61' in his songs?

DID YOU KNOW?
Of the Top 20 best-selling UK singles in the Sixties, seven were by The Beatles.

Quiz 3

The Seventies

Lest we forget, 'the decade that taste forgot' also brought you glam rock and metal, disco and punk ...

Answers page 222

1. In 1971, a gig by Frank Zappa and the Mothers of Invention abruptly ended when a fan's flare gun started a fire at the venue – Montreux Casino in Switzerland. Which Deep Purple song chronicles the event?
    a) 'Black Night'
    b) 'Fireball'
    c) 'Smoke on the Water'

2. Rod Stewart's single 'Maggie May' and parent album *Every Picture Tells a Story* achieved something even The Beatles hadn't managed. What?

3. Which guitarist played with David Bowie from the albums *The Man Who Sold the World* (1970) to *Pin Ups* (1973)?
    a) Mick Ronson
    b) Mick Taylor
    c) Mick Jones

4. Patti Smith recorded an incendiary cover of 'Gloria' for her debut album *Horses* (1975). Who wrote the original garage-rock classic it was based on?

5. Name the high-flying group that Lionel Richie was in before he went solo.

6. The *Daily Mirror* of 2 December 1976 bore the headline 'The Filth and the Fury!' There had been an expletive-spattered TV interview by a band on the previous night. Name them.

7. Which classic 1973 album originally featured a sleeve designed to look like a Zippo lighter?

8. What was the first UK punk single to be released?

9. Piqued at being turned away from New York's celebrated club Studio 54, songwriters Nile Rodgers and Bernard Edwards penned a narky riposte provisionally titled 'Fuck Off!' By what name is this disco classic better known?
    a) 'Le Freak'
    b) 'Good Times'
    c) 'Machine Gun'

10. **What did the initials of key New York punk club CBGB stand for?**
a) Chico, Billy, Gerry and Bob
b) Chains, Bombs, Guns and Bullets
c) Country, BlueGrass and Blues

11. **Who wrote the soundtrack for the classic Blaxploitation movie *Super Fly* (1972)?**

12. **By what name were teen idols Eric, Woody, Les, Alan and Derek better known?**
a) The Osmonds
b) Bay City Rollers
c) The Glitter Band

13. **What was T. Rex's first UK No.1?**
a) 'Get It On'
b) 'Hot Love'
c) 'Telegram Sam'

14. **Which 1977 hit song, featuring a celebrated guitar coda, was originally titled 'Mexican Reggae'?**

15. **Which Latin American first lady was the subject of the 1976 UK No.1 'Don't Cry For Me Argentina'?**

16. **In which year did ABBA win the Eurovision Song Contest?**
a) 1972
b) 1973
c) 1974

SAY WHAT?

'That's it. Period. I don't want to do any more gigs, and all the American dates have been cancelled. From now on, I'll be concentrating on various activities that have very little to do with rock and pop.' David Bowie, on his 'retirement' from music. It didn't last long ... (*NME*, 7 July 1973)

Quiz 4

The Eighties

The decade that saw the rise of rap, rave and poodle rock. Michael Jackson was crowned the King of Pop and Band Aid proved that rock had a conscience.

Answers page 223

1. The riff from Killing Joke's song 'Eighties' (1984) had an audible influence on a 1990s hit for another band. Who were that band and their song?

2. Which Madonna video was inspired by Fritz Lang, director of silent movie *Metropolis* (1927)?
   a) 'Vogue'
   b) 'Like a Prayer'
   c) 'Express Yourself'

3. Keeping with *Metropolis*, scenes from the film featured in the video for which 1984 Queen song?

4. Which Frankie Goes To Hollywood single was banned in 1984?

5. Which James Bond film featured Grace Jones?
   a) *For Your Eyes Only* (1981)
   b) *A View to a Kill* (1985)
   c) *The Living Daylights* (1987)

6. In which metal band was Cliff Burton the original bassist?

7. Released in 1984, this colourful album went 13 times platinum, spawned five hit singles (including two US No.1s) and remains the third best-selling soundtrack LP ever. What is it?

8. This legendary Sixties singer wigged out as an actress in *Mad Max: Beyond Thunderdome* (1985). Who is she?
   a) Sandy Shaw
   b) Grace Slick
   c) Tina Turner

9. Michael Jackson's all-conquering *Thriller* (1984) album has sold in excess of 66 million copies worldwide and spawned seven *Billboard* Top 10 singles. Name four of them.

10. Band Aid's charity single 'Do They Know It's Christmas?' was a mega-selling festive No.1 in the UK. Meanwhile, in the USA star musicians collaborated on their own single for the same cause. What were they called – and what was the single?

11. **What was the name of Guns N' Roses' only *Billboard* No.1 single?**
    a) 'Sweet Emotion'
    b) 'Sweet Home Alabama'
    c) 'Sweet Child o' Mine'

12. **Public Enemy's most commercially successful LP was considered significant enough to be preserved in the Library of Congress. What was it?**
    a) *Yo! Bum Rush the Show* (1987)
    b) *It Takes a Nation of Millions to Hold Us Back* (1988)
    c) *Fear of a Black Planet* (1989)

13. **Inspired by South African township music, Paul Simon's best-selling LP won a Grammy in 1987. What was it called?**

14. ***Squirrel and G-Man Twenty Four Hour Party People Plastic Face Carnt Smile (White Out)* was the title of whose 1987 debut LP?**

15. **When did the Rock and Roll Hall of Fame open its doors?**
    a) 1984
    b) 1986
    c) 1988

16. **Which 1989 LP announced the birth of the D.A.I.S.Y. Age?**

DID YOU KNOW?

Phil Collins was the only artist to appear at both the UK and US Live Aid concerts in 1985. He flew from London to Philadelphia via Concorde.

Quiz 5

The
Nineties

Britpop took hold of the UK charts, spearheaded
by Blur and Oasis, while grunge dominated Stateside
rock and hip hop diversified. But can you tell your
Spice Girls from your All Saints?

Answers page 224

1. Their first two albums were *A Storm in Heaven* (1993) and *A Northern Soul* (1995), but their third – released in 1997 – became a multi-platinum best-seller and UK No.1. Name the band and that album.

2. Snoop Dogg scored a US No.1 with his 1993 debut album. Name it.

3. Which rapper guested on Sonic Youth's 1990 single 'Kool Thing'?

4. In what year did Prince change his name to a symbol?
   a) 1993
   b) 1995
   c) 1997

5. Ambient house anthem 'Little Fluffy Clouds' was a UK Top 10 single in 1991. It included samples of a 1970s singer-songwriter remembering the skies of her childhood. Who was she?

6. Nirvana's album *Nevermind* (1991) hit No.1 on *Billboard* on 11 January 1992. Which album did it displace?
   a) *Achtung Baby*, by U2
   b) *Dangerous*, by Michael Jackson
   c) *Ropin' the Wind*, by Garth Brooks

7. Having topped the UK charts for three months in 1994, Wet Wet Wet decided to withdraw their ubiquitous single from sale. What was its title?

8. Brothers Taylor, Zac and Isaac made up which band?

9. When did *Billboard* begin to record sales of downloads?
   a) 1994
   b) 1996
   c) 1998

10. Who were 'Sorted for E's and Wizz' in 1995?

11. **Spice Girls topped the UK charts with their first six singles. True or false?**

12. **What is Brian Warner's shock-rock alter ego?**

13. **Name Prince's sole UK No.1.**
    a) 'My Name Is Prince'
    b) 'Controversy'
    c) 'The Most Beautiful Girl in the World'

14. **Guitarist Carlos Santana enjoyed a mega-successful comeback album in 1999, racking up sales of 25 million copies worldwide and netting five Grammys. What was the otherworldly name of the record?**

15. **What 1997 girl-group hit was based on the traditional Christian hymn 'Amazing Grace'?**

16. **Which band recorded 'I'll Be There for You', the *Friends* theme tune, in 1994?**
    a) The Rembrandts
    b) The Picassos
    c) The Turners

SAY WHAT?
'I've listened to the Oasis CD but it doesn't appeal to me. I know everyone's into them in Britain but everyone listens to Mariah Carey here and I'm not into that either.' Madonna (*NME*, 2 December 1995)

Quiz 6

The New Millennium

The inexorable rise of rap continues – spectacularly so in the case of Drake's chart success. Meanwhile, megastars such as Beyoncé and Taylor Swift redefine the parameters of pop.

Answers page 225

1.   Which band once considered calling themselves
      The Genius Sex Poets?

2.   As of January 2019, what is the most viewed music video
      on YouTube?
      a) 'Despacito', by Luis Fonsi feat. Daddy Yankee
      b) 'Shake It Off', by Taylor Swift
      c) 'Hello', by Adele

3.   Which two-piece rock group wore only red, white or black?

4.   Which rapper went straight in at No.1 on *Billboard* with his
      debut album (the best-selling US LP of 2003) *and* became the
      first artist to have three simultaneous hits in the US Top 5?

5.   In 2013, Eminem's 'Rap God' set a new world record. What for?
      a) Fastest time to sell 5 million copies
      b) Shortest No.1 single
      c) Most words in a hit single

6.   'Unchained Melody' was a hit in the 1950s and 1960s for
      various artists, including The Righteous Brothers. Who scored
      the biggest-selling UK single of the 2000s with it?

7.   Who is currently the highest-earning female pop star?
      a) Beyoncé
      b) Taylor Swift
      c) Katy Perry

8.   Who asked us to 'Take Me Out' in 2004?

9.   In July 2014, one artist became the first person on Facebook
      to attract 100 million likes. Who was it?
      a) Jay-Z
      b) Kanye West
      c) Shakira

10.   In 2016, one artist became the first act to have the top three
      singles on the UK charts. Who was it?
      a) Justin Bieber
      b) Taylor Swift
      c) Drake

11. They had their first UK No.1 album – its title taken from Alan Sillitoe's classic novel *Saturday Night and Sunday Morning* – in 2006. It became the UK's fastest-selling debut LP by a band. Every one of its five successors has also topped the British charts. Who are they?

12. One artist has spent an unprecedented 431 consecutive weeks on the *Billboard* Hot 100. Who is it?
     a) Drake
     b) Taylor Swift
     c) Jay-Z

13. What milestone for views did Psy's video for 'Gangnam Style' (2012) achieve?

14. What is the best-selling digital single?
     a) 'Uptown Funk', by Mark Ronson feat. Bruno Mars
     b) 'Call Me Maybe', by Carly Rae Jepsen
     c) 'Rolling in the Deep', by Adele

15. One artist has now had No.1 *Billboard* 200 albums over six decades. Name that singer.

16. What unprecedented feat did Bruno Mars achieve with the singles 'Just the Way You Are' (2010), 'Grenade' (2010) and 'Uptown Funk' (2014)?
     a) They were all simultaneous UK and US No.1s
     b) All three singles sold 10 million copies worldwide
     c) All three were No.1s for him before

DID YOU KNOW?
In 2014, digital music sales overtook physical sales for the first time.

GENRES

Quiz 1

Lively Up Yourself

Reggae, Jamaica's gift to the world,
spread inspirational joy, righteous anger
against Babylon and sweet ganja fumes.
And all to that signature offbeat.

Answers page 226

1. Which reggae band released an acclaimed album called *Marcus Garvey* in 1975, after the Jamaican cultural icon and Rastafarian prophet?
   a) Burning Spear
   b) Aswad
   c) Steel Pulse

2. Which British band designed the cover of their 1980 debut album to look like a government unemployment benefit form?

3. Born Horace Swaby, he recorded the classic dub album *King Tubbys Meets Rockers Uptown* in 1976. By what name is he better known?

4. Which British guitar god had a US No.1 with a cover of Bob Marley's 'I Shot the Sheriff' in 1974?
   a) Jeff Beck
   b) Eric Clapton
   c) Mick Taylor

5. Where was the famous live version of Bob Marley and the Wailers' 'No Woman, No Cry' recorded?
   a) Madison Square Garden, New York
   b) Lyceum Theatre, London
   c) Lesser Free Trade Hall, Manchester

6. One British reggae outfit named their debut album *Handsworth Revolution* (1978), after the district in the Midlands where they were born. Name the band.
   a) UB40
   b) Eclipse
   c) Steel Pulse

7. Which notable first did Black Uhuru achieve with their album *Anthem*?
   a) First reggae album to sell over 5 million copies
   b) First US *Billboard* 200 No.1
   c) First winner of the Grammy for Best Reggae Album

8. The Clash covered 'Police and Thieves' on their titular debut album in 1977. Who sang the original?

9. This singular producer oversaw key recordings by Bob Marley and the Wailers, The Congos, The Upsetters and Max Romeo, among others. His backyard studio, the Black Ark, burned down in uncertain circumstances. Name him.

10. Who took 'Uptown Top Ranking' to the top of the UK singles chart in 1977?

11. Who had a big lovers-rock hit in 1979 with 'Silly Games'?
    a) Minnie Riperton
    b) Janis Ian
    c) Janet Kay

12. 'Do the Reggay' is widely accepted as the first pop song to use 'reggae' in its title. Who recorded it?
    a) The Skatalites
    b) Toots and the Maytals
    c) The Heptones

13. Who had a hit with 'You Don't Love Me (No, No, No)' in 1994?

14. Which weed-loving ex-Wailer's debut solo album was entitled *Legalize It*?

15. The Paragons' 'The Tide Is High' was a transatlantic No.1 in 1980 – for who?

16. Boney M covered a song by The Melodians that had originally appeared on the soundtrack for *The Harder They Come* (1972) and took it to No.1 in the UK in 1978. It is still one of the top ten best-selling singles of all time in the UK. What was the track?

SAY WHAT?

'The song is about the strength in the mama, of course, strength in the ladies. And we love a woman with a backbone. Something like a wishbone! They have to be like a she lion!' Wailers bass player Aston 'Family Man' Barrett on 'No Woman, No Cry' (*NME*, 30 June 2012)

Quiz 2

Never Mind the Bollocks

The mid-Seventies offered slim pickings for the musical gourmand. The *menu du jour* featured bland, family-friendly cheese or an overinflated prog-rock soufflé. Those hungry for change opted for street food: punk.

Answers page 227

1. **What was the first single by Sex Pistols?**
    a) 'Anarchy in the UK'
    b) 'God Save the Queen'
    c) 'Pretty Vacant'

2. **The Clash had to wait until 1991 for their only UK No.1 – when it featured in a jeans advert. What was it?**

3. **Which Mancunian punk band self-released the hugely influential four-track *Spiral Scratch* EP?**

4. **He was backed by the Voidoids, approached by Malcolm McLaren to front Sex Pistols and wrote the proto-punk song 'Blank Generation'. Name him.**

5. **Which controversial West Coast punk band took a 'Holiday in Cambodia' but were 'Too Drunk to Fuck'?**

6. **The Damned's 1976 debut single, 'New Rose', is widely regarded as the first UK punk single. What Beatles song did they cover on the B-side?**
    a) 'Help!'
    b) 'Revolution'
    c) 'A Hard Day's Night'

7. **What was the name of future Pogue Shane MacGowan's punk band?**
    a) The Broken Bones
    b) The Ear Bleeders
    c) The Nipple Erectors

8. **Which influential punk band included Ari Up and Palmolive?**

9. **Which classic punk hit single namechecked Leon Trotsky and Sancho Panza?**

10. **'Beat on the Brat', 'Now I Wanna Sniff Some Glue' and 'I Don't Wanna Go Down to the Basement' appear on which eponymous punk debut album?**

11. The Heartbreakers' guitarist Johnny Thunders and drummer Jerry Nolan had been in a glam/hard-rock band beforehand – one of Morrissey's favourite artists, no less. What were they called?
a) Sparks
b) Rocket from the Tombs
c) New York Dolls

12. Pat Smear of Germs went on to play with one of the biggest bands of the 1990s. Who were they?
a) Oasis
b) Nirvana
c) Green Day

13. The riff from Wire's 'Three Girl Rhumba' was appropriated by Elastica for which Top 20 UK hit in 1994?
a) 'Waking Up'
b) 'Stutter'
c) 'Connection'

14. Before becoming Sex Pistols' bassist in 1977, Sid Vicious had already appeared as the drummer with another famous British punk band. Name them.

15. Which band's early releases included 'Suspect Device', 'Alternative Ulster' and *Inflammable Material*?

16. Which band did Poly Styrene front?

SAY WHAT?
'Actually we're not into music ... We're into chaos.'
Steve Jones of Sex Pistols (*NME*, 21 February 1976)

Quiz 3

Burn This Disco Down

When the going gets tough, the tough go dancing. Born in loft parties and clubs in a New York City then down on its knees, disco was all over the charts by the late Seventies. Highbrows and 'serious' artists dismissed it all as mindless hedonism – rather missing the point.

Answers page 228

1. Which smooth-talking Seventies star was dubbed the 'Walrus of Love'?

2. Carl Douglas had the best-selling single of 1974 (and a UK/US No.1) with a song about martial arts. Name it.

3. In 1980 – for one year only – the Grammys had an award for Best Disco Performance. What song won it?
   a) 'Don't Stop 'Til You Get Enough', by Michael Jackson
   b) 'Boogie Wonderland', by Earth, Wind and Fire
   c) 'I Will Survive', by Gloria Gaynor

4. Who produced Donna Summer's 1977 synth-disco smash 'I Feel Love'?
   a) George Martin
   b) Giorgio Moroder
   c) Nile Rodgers and Bernard Edwards

5. Which disco soundtrack yielded eight US No.1 singles (and six Grammys)?

6. Which newspaper do the Bee Gees namecheck in 'Stayin' Alive'?

7. Who declared 'We Are Family' in 1979?
   a) The Pointer Sisters
   b) Sister Sledge
   c) Twisted Sister

8. The bassline from which song inspired Queen's John Deacon to write 'Another One Bites the Dust'?
   a) 'Good Times', by Chic
   b) 'Ball of Confusion', by The Temptations
   c) 'Shaft', by Isaac Hayes

9. Who had a 'Love Hangover' in 1976?

10. Labelle's 1974 US No.1 'Lady Marmalade' was covered in 2001 by Christina Aguilera, Mýa, Pink and Lil' Kim for a movie soundtrack. What was the movie?

11. 'I'm Your Boogie Man', 'Queen of Clubs', '(Shake, Shake, Shake) Shake Your Booty' and 'That's the Way (I Like It)' were all hits for which act?

12. Which hard-rock band went disco with 'I Was Made for Lovin' You' (1979)?
    a) Judas Priest
    b) Rainbow
    c) Kiss

13. What was The Trammps' scorching disco hit?
    a) 'Fire'
    b) 'Disco Inferno'
    c) 'Hot Stuff'

14. 'Dancing Queen' (1976) was ABBA's sole *Billboard* No.1 single. True or false?

15. The soundtrack for the movie *Car Wash* (1976) was the debut album of a band who also scored a US No.1 with the title song. Who were they?

16. What event – often credited with marking disco's demise – took place in Chicago's Comiskey Park on 12 July 1979?
    a) A concert featuring Chic, Sister Sledge and Sylvester sold less than half the available tickets
    b) Thousands of disco records were destroyed in 'Disco Demolition Night'
    c) Donna Summer publicly disowned the genre, citing its immoral undertones

DID YOU KNOW?
Bianca Jagger rode a white horse across the dance floor of legendary disco club Studio 54 on her 30th birthday in 1977.

Quiz 4

Rock'n'Roll Ain't Noise Pollution

Born in the Sixties, metal came of age in the Seventies, then spawned a hydra-like plethora of subgenres and hybrids, from thrash to Nineties nu metal and deathcore. Play this quiz at maximum volume.

Answers page 229

1. Which bands were dubbed the 'Unholy Trinity of Heavy Metal'?

2. In 2016, Bring Me the Horizon's lead singer, Oliver Sykes, leapt on to a table at the NME Awards and proceeded to trash it. Which band were at the table?
   a) Arctic Monkeys
   b) Coldplay
   c) Muse

3. It went 10 times platinum in the States alone, but which band recorded *Pyromania* (1983)?

4. Which Led Zeppelin album features the Giant's Causew: in County Antrim, Northern Ireland, on the cover?

5. Which of the following lead singers is also a qualified pilot?
   a) Ian Gillan
   b) Jon Bon Jovi
   c) Bruce Dickinson

6. Who replaced Ozzy Osbourne as Black Sabbath's vocalist in 1979?
   a) Graham Bonnet
   b) Ian Gillan
   c) Ronnie James Dio

7. How many copies has AC/DC's album *Back in Black* (1980) sold?
   a) 10 million
   b) 30 million
   c) 50 million

8. Which Guns N' Roses album placed higher on the *Billboard* 200, *Use Your Illusion I* or *Use Your Illusion II*?

9. Which quartet of bands are known as the 'Big Four of Thrash Metal'?

10. Complete the Motörhead album title: *No Sleep 'til —.*
    a) *Brooklyn*
    b) *Hell*
    c) *Hammersmith*

11. Which hedonistic duo were known as the 'Toxic Twins'?

12. Who produced Slayer's landmark 1986 album *Reign in Blood*?
    a) Rick Rubin
    b) Flemming Rasmussen
    c) Bob Rock

13. Who recorded the LP *British Steel* in 1980?

14. *Hybrid Theory* (2000) became the fastest-selling rock LP since Guns N' Roses' *Appetite for Destruction,* reaching No.2 on the *Billboard* 200 and shifting in excess of 11 million copies. Who was the artist?

15. They wear distinctive masks, scored their first US No.1 album with *All Hope Is Gone* (2008) and have their own clothing brand called 'Tattered and Torn'. Who are they?

16. 'Sweet Dreams (Are Made of This)', 'Tainted Love' and 'Personal Jesus' were all covered by which artist?

DID YOU KNOW?
Black Sabbath named themselves after a 1963 horror movie starring Boris Karloff.

Quiz 5

Straight Outta Compton

Initially dismissed as a novelty, hip hop has proved remarkably resilient and adaptable, embracing everything from Public Enemy's hardcore politics, Wu-Tang Clan's dizzying diversity, Kanye West's inventive productions and all points in-between. But can you tell your Eazy-E from your Jay-Z?

Answers page 230

1. They recorded hard-hitting social commentary tunes such as 'The Message' and 'White Lines' and became the first hip hop group to be inducted into the Rock and Roll Hall of Fame. Name them.

2. Which Blondie song namechecks Fab Five Freddy?

3. For which movie was Public Enemy's 'Fight the Power' written?
   a) *Boyz n the Hood*
   b) *Malcolm X*
   c) *Do the Right Thing*

4. Name any three members of Wu-Tang Clan, past or present.

5. Beastie Boys' debut album went 10 times platinum in the USA. What was its title?
   a) *Ill Communication*
   b) *Licensed to Ill*
   c) *To the 5 Boroughs*

6. 'The Magic Number', 'Me Myself and I' and 'Ring Ring Ring (Ha Ha Hey)' were all singles by which hip hop trio?

7. Which member of NWA left the band after their blistering and insanely controversial debut *Straight Outta Compton* (1988)?
   a) Dr. Dre
   b) Eazy-E
   c) Ice Cube

8. The first hip hop album to receive a diamond certification in the USA (for sales of 10 million plus) featured the hit single 'U Can't Touch This'. Name the artist.

9. She's sold in excess of 15 million albums and 30 million singles. Her best-known tracks include 'Big Momma Thang' and 'Not Tonight'. Her best-known feud is with Nicki Minaj. Who is she?

10. As a group member, she enjoyed multi-platinum success with *The Score* (1996) before going on to shift 19 million copies with her debut solo album. Who is she?

11. Iconic rappers Christopher George Latore Wallace and Lesane Parish Crooks were key figures in the East Coast–West Coast hip hop rivalry of the 1990s. By what names are they better known?

12. Featuring ground-breaking productions by Timbaland, she racked up hit albums and singles including 'One Minute Man', 'Get Ur Freak On' and 'Work It'. Name her.

13. Who has scored the most *Billboard* 200 No.1 albums by a solo artist?
    a) Jay-Z
    b) Eminem
    c) 50 Cent

14. 'Hey Ya!' held the US No.1 spot for nine weeks, replaced by 'The Way You Move'. Both were taken from the double album *Speakerboxxx/The Love Below* (2003). Name the act.

15. Kendrick Lamar's 2015 album debuted at the No.1 spot in both the UK and the USA. What was it called?

16. 'The mob can't make me not love him ... We are both dragon energy. He is my brother.' Who was Kanye West enthusing about in April 2018?

DID YOU KNOW?
In 2017, Forbes reported that hip hop had overtaken rock as America's most popular genre of music.

Quiz 6

Cigarettes and Alcohol

Bristling at the wave of grunge from the States in the early Nineties, UK bands fought back with defiantly home-grown ammo (glam rock, mod and punk). Was Britpop slack revivalism or vibrant reinvention? And while you're asking yourself that, ask yourself this ...

Answers page 231

1. **What do Oasis's *Definitely Maybe* (1994) and Elastica's *Elastica* (1995) have in common?**
   a) Both sold more than 5 million copies
   b) Both were the fastest-selling debut album in the UK for a time
   c) Both returned to the No.1 spot after initially topping the charts

2. **What was Oasis's first UK No.1?**
   a) 'Wonderwall'
   b) 'Roll with It'
   c) 'Some Might Say'

3. **In which city did Pulp form?**
   a) Manchester
   b) Leicester
   c) Sheffield

4. **Who were 'Caught by the Fuzz' in 1994?**

5. **Elastica's 'Waking Up' sounded so much like one particular Stranglers tune that they had to make an out-of-court settlement with the old punks. What was the source song?**
   a) 'Something Better Change'
   b) 'No More Heroes'
   c) 'Duchess'

6. **Which Britpop album featured a painting of the famous Mallard steam train on its cover?**

7. **Which artist sang to us about 'Babies', 'Joyriders' and 'Bar Italia' while advising 'Help the Aged'?**
   a) Echobelly
   b) Pulp
   c) Cast

8. **The same band's final album was produced by a singer whose ship definitely came in during the 1960s. Name him.**
   a) Tom Jones
   b) Scott Walker
   c) Joe Cocker

9. What design adorned both Noel Gallagher's guitar and Geri Halliwell's dress?

10. Suede's original guitarist quit after completing their second album, *Dog Man Star* (1994). Name him.

11. Which Manic Street Preachers song opened with a celebration of public libraries?
    a) 'You Love Us'
    b) 'Kevin Carter'
    c) 'A Design for Life'

12. The Verve's song 'History' was inspired by the poem *London* – written by which revered English poet?
    a) Lord Byron
    b) William Blake
    c) John Keats

13. Neil Young's 1968 song 'Expecting to Fly' shared its title with the 1996 debut LP of which band?

14. Which cult band had John Power been in before he formed Cast?

15. For which band did Sonya Madan sing?

16. Naming themselves after a character in Harper Lee's novel *To Kill a Mockingbird* (1960), this band made giant steps in 1993. Who were they?

SAY WHAT?
'Prince William is a Pulp fan, you know. "One wants to live with the common people ..." Good name to have on the guest list, though.'
Jarvis Cocker of Pulp (*NME*, 23 December 1995)

Quiz 7

Eat, Sleep, Rave, Repeat

The rise of house music and warehouse parties in the late 1980s had an incalculable effect on club culture and pop, with elements of dubstep, trance and house infiltrating dance music and the charts. Let's take a trip – and it *is* a trip – through the rise and rise of bpms.

Answers page 232

1. David Bowie recalled Brian Eno telling him during the late 1970s in Berlin, '"I have heard the sound of the future ... This single is going to change the sound of club music for the next 15 years." Which was more or less right.' What was the song?
    a) 'I Feel Love', by Donna Summer
    b) 'Oxygène IV', by Jean-Michel Jarre
    c) 'Being Boiled', by The Human League

2. In 2013, *The Observer* newspaper commented that 'No other band since The Beatles has given so much to pop culture'. Name that model group.

3. Who advised us to 'Pump Up the Volume' in 1987?

4. Samples from TZ's 'I Got the Hots for You' and Rose Royce's 'Is It Love You're After' featured prominently in a 1988 acid house UK No.1. What was it?

5. The tune 'Strings of Life' is a key track in the histories of house and techno. It was credited to Rhythim Is Rhythim, but what was the real name of the producer behind it?
    a) Derrick May
    b) Frankie Knuckles
    c) Steve 'Silk' Hurley

6. By what name are brothers Phil and Paul Hartnoll better known? And for a bonus point, what inspired their name?

7. Who released the critically acclaimed albums *dubnobasswithmyheadman* (1994) and *Second Toughest in the Infants* (1996)?

8. Who went 'Around the World' in 1997, 'Harder, Better, Faster, Stronger' in 2001 and got lucky in 2013?

9. When The Prodigy and Beastie Boys both played Reading Festival in 1998, the Beasties asked the UK act to remove one number from their set. The Prodigy ignored them. What was the offending song?

10. Whose 1997 remix of Run-DMC's 'It's Like That' became a UK No.1?

11. Which drum and bass artist recorded the 21-minute orchestral epic 'Inner City Life' in 1995, appeared in the 1997 James Bond movie *The World Is Not Enough* and wound up with an MBE in 2016?

12. Which superstar DJs had to change their original pseudonym – The Dust Brothers – because it clashed with the name of US producers who had already worked with Beck and Beastie Boys?

13. Sonny John Moore holds the record for the electronic dance music act with the most Grammys (eight). By what name is he better known?
    a) David Guetta
    b) Lindstrøm
    c) Skrillex

14. In what year did the Grammys introduce a category for Best Electronic/Dance Album?
    a) 1995
    b) 2000
    c) 2005

15. From 2013 to 2017, one artist was the highest-paid DJ on the planet, according to Forbes. Among other achievements, he became the first artist to score nine UK Top 10 hits from one album – beating a record previously held by Michael Jackson. Who is he?

16. Grammy-nominated EDM artist Joel Thomas Zimmerman wears a distinctive mask when performing. He's not taking the mickey, though. What is his stage name?

SAY WHAT?

'I don't know the EDM artists or the albums. At first I thought it was all just one guy, some DJ called EDM.' Guy-Manuel de Homem-Christo of Daft Punk (*NME*, 14 May 2013)

Quiz 8

Grime Wave

Born in east London council estates at the start
of the new millennium, grime was initially considered
outsider, underdog music. But its shape-shifting
breakbeats and lyrics addressing hard times
and social deprivation swiftly found it a national and
then international audience. Under its umbrella,
home-grown rappers have become global names.

Answers page 233

1. Tinchy Stryder, Dizzee Rascal and Skepta all belonged to which crew?

2. What song gave So Solid Crew a UK No.1 in 2001?

3. What was Kano's debut single?

4. The first single by the More Fire Crew collective made No.7 in the UK in 2002, one of grime's biggest hits. Name it.

5. What is the name of Jammer's series of annual rap contests (also released on DVD), created as a platform for up-and-coming grime artists?

6. Which two grime artists have scored Mercury Music Prizes? And for a bonus point, name the albums that won them the award.

7. Who was the first grime artist to score a UK No.1 album – and what was it?

8. Beginning in 2015, Bugzy Malone engaged in a well-publicized feud with which fellow rapper?

9. What was the title of the critically acclaimed debut album by The Streets (aka Mike Skinner)?

10. A 2004 single by Lethal Bizzle became a UK No.11 hit, but was also banned from some clubs for its tendency to incite violence on the dance floor. Name it.

11. Who is Skepta's younger brother?

12. In 2005, one of Rinse FM's founders was given an ASBO banning him from the roof of any building higher than four storeys in the London borough of Tower Hamlets. Name him.

13. In 2006, which leading politician wrote an article for the *Mail on Sunday* entitled 'You're talking rubbish, Lethal Bizzle'?

14. In 2015, who shared the stage at the BRITs with a crew including home-grown MCs Skepta, Stormzy, Novelist and Jammer, among others?

15. Which record-breaking rapper signed to Boy Better Know in 2016?

16. Which grime pioneer was awarded an MBE in 2018 for services to music?

SAY WHAT?

'We've been ahead for so long in the UK, we're so multicultural and that's the beauty ... That's why grime was formed, from this mix, this understanding of different people. Now other people are catching on. There's a revolution happening.' Skepta (*The Guardian*, 10 September 2016)

CONTROVERSY

Quiz 1

Live and Dangerous

Unpredictable artists can bring a whole lot more
to a gig than just the music and light show.
From fights to feathered friends in peril, how well
do you know your in-concert dramas?

Answers page 234

1. Who bit the head off a bat onstage in 1982?

2. What happened to a chicken during Alice Cooper's set at
    the Rock and Roll Revival concert in Toronto in 1969?
    a) It settled on the drum kit and stayed there for the whole set
    b) It defecated on Alice's shoes
    c) He threw it into the audience, who ripped it apart

3. At a 1973 concert, fan Scot Halpin was recruited from the
    audience to help complete the set when the band's drummer
    collapsed. Name the band.

4. An infamous 'wardrobe malfunction' led to the exposure
    of a singer's breast during the Superbowl half-time break
    in 2004. Who was she? And for a bonus point, who was she
    duetting with at the time?

5. The closing date of The Rolling Stones' 1969 US tour ended
    in tragedy, when a fan was killed by Hells Angels during the
    concert. Where was it held?
    a) Altamont Speedway, California
    b) Madison Square Garden, New York
    c) Fillmore West, California

6. What was Jim Morrison accused of doing at a Doors concert
    in 1969, resulting in his arrest and a court case?
    a) Assaulting a policeman onstage
    b) Exposing himself
    c) Attacking a member of the audience

7. A riot broke out at a 1981 Public Image Ltd gig at the Ritz club
    in New York. What got the fans mad?
    a) The band refused to come onstage
    b) Frontman John Lydon wouldn't sing
    c) The band performed behind a screen

8. Who was brought onstage in a wheelchair at Reading Festival
    in 1992 – deliberately parodying reports of his fragile health
    – before delivering a blistering set with his band?

9. **Criticized for appearing at 2008's Glastonbury by Noel Gallagher, Jay-Z cheekily strolled onstage and started singing an Oasis song. Which one?**
   a) 'Live Forever'
   b) 'Wonderwall'
   c) 'Don't Look Back in Anger'

10. **What enraged fans during Bob Dylan's appearance at the Newport Folk Festival in July 1965?**
    a) He played completely different arrangements of his classic songs
    b) He turned his back on the audience for the entire set
    c) He and his band 'went electric', using electric guitars and amplifiers for the first time

11. **What did MIA. do while onstage during Madonna's 2012 Superbowl performance that upset some viewers?**
    a) She mouthed an expletive at the camera
    b) She flipped a middle finger at the camera
    c) She tore a small 'Stars and Stripes' flag in half

12. **Which singer ripped up a photo of the Pope during a live performance on *Saturday Night Live* in 1992?**

13. **Which rapper wore a hockey mask and sported a chainsaw for some of his early 2000s gigs?**

14. **How did The Stranglers cause controversy at a gig in London's Battersea Park in 1978?**
    a) They destroyed their instruments before they'd even begun
    b) They wore joke shop masks for the whole set
    c) They were accompanied by strippers for one song

15. **In 2016, Beyoncé's memorable Superbowl half-time performance attracted protests from some critics (and plaudits from many others). Why?**

16. **Who ended a legendary set during a 1967 concert at Monterey in California by setting fire to his guitar and then smashing it?**
    a) Pete Townshend
    b) Jimi Hendrix
    c) Eric Clapton

Quiz 2

Excess All Areas

In the past, most self-respecting rock stars could list 'general debauchery' on their CV. Overindulgence came with the territory, spawned legends, filled newspaper columns and sometimes ended in court.

Answers page 235

1. Serge Gainsbourg livened up a French chat show in 1986 by telling a fellow guest that he'd like to fuck her. Who was the lucky lady?

2. In 1976, a true rock'n'roll legend was arrested for driving drunk. Scant hours later – and now toting a loaded gun – he arrived at Graceland, Elvis Presley's home, demanding to see the singer (he was refused entry). Who was it?
   a) Little Richard
   b) Jerry Lee Lewis
   c) Carl Perkins

3. In 2007, one unfortunate male escort found himself manacled to a radiator and beaten with a chain (yes, cocaine was involved). Someone really wanted to hurt him – but who?

4. In a contest between Ozzy Osbourne and Mötley Crüe's Nikki Sixx to decide who could out rock'n'roll the other, Sixx set himself on fire. How did Ozzy respond?
   a) He threw himself out of a fourth-storey apartment
   b) He glugged down three bottles of whisky
   c) He snorted a line of ants

5. One renowned producer held one gun to Leonard Cohen's head and fired another in the studio during a John Lennon session. Who was he?

6. Prior to a concert in Michigan Palace, Detroit, one flamboyant singer challenged a local biker gang to a fight. During the gig, the bikers pelted him with everything from urine to broken glass, only for the band to wind them up further by playing a 45-minute version of 'Louie Louie'. Finally, the singer called out one biker in particular, confronted him in the audience ... and was beaten up. Quite a day's work. The gig was recorded and released as an album. Who was the singer?

7. One loony drummer had a penchant for dropping explosives down toilets, resulting in him being banned from all Holiday Inns in the USA and a range of other hotels. Name him.

8. Which member of Guns N' Roses was arrested in 1989 after openly urinating in an aeroplane mid-flight because he couldn't be bothered to wait for the toilet?

9. In 1982, while in San Antonio, Texas, this drunk singer urinated on a cenotaph erected in memory of those who fell at the Alamo. He was wearing one of his wife's dresses at the time. Who was he?
a) David Lee Roth
b) Ozzy Osbourne
c) Alice Cooper

10. Which singer dangled his own child from the balcony of a hotel room in 2002?

11. In 1977, *NME* journalist Tony Parsons interviewed one band as they boozed and snorted speed while travelling on a London Tube line. Who were they?

12. To avoid damaging his nose from excessive drug snorting, Rod Stewart gave himself cocaine suppositories instead. True or false?

13. Partying hard in Bangkok's Oriental Hotel in 1989, one rock star incurred a bill of hundreds of thousands of dollars. Then, on refusing to vacate the premises, he was shot with a tranquilizer dart and removed on a stretcher by soldiers. He certainly made it hot in the city ... But who was he?

14. Cocaine use was so prevalent at the recording sessions for one mega-selling Seventies album that the band in question considered including their dealer in the credits. Name the band – and, for a bonus point, name the album.

15. Ah, the Seventies! At the notoriously bohemian launch party for one album, guests were greeted by dwarves with trays of top-drawer cocaine strapped to their heads. The entertainment included a man who bit the heads off live chickens (no, not Ozzy), transsexual strippers, naked dancers in bamboo cages and nude wrestling in a pit of liver ... Name the band. And for an extra point, what was the album in question?

16. When the wife of country singer George Jones – then an infamous booze hound – hid his car keys to stop him driving into town for more drink, how did George get around the problem?
a) He had it delivered to the house
b) He rode a horse into town
c) He rode a lawnmower into town

Quiz 3

Can't Say That on the Radio

The powers that be (hello, BBC) used to take a dim view of anything whiffing of scandal and ban it before it could reach innocent ears. Needless to say, that often only boosted sales ...

Answers page 236

1. Why was The Who's 1965 teen anthem 'My Generation' banned?

2. The Kinks' 1970 hit 'Lola' was banned because of references to transvestism in the lyrics. True or false?

3. Pink Floyd's debut single 'Arnold Layne' was banned because of references to transvestism in the lyrics. True or false?

4. Why was John Leyton's 'Johnny Remember Me' (1961) banned by the BBC?

5. Heaven 17's '(We Don't Need This) Fascist Groove Thang' included lyrics that the BBC felt might libel a US president. They pulled it from the airwaves – but who was the Leader of the Free World in question?
   a) Jimmy Carter
   b) Ronald Reagan
   c) Bill Clinton

6. This Radiohead song was originally banned because it was thought to be too depressing. And it contained the 'f' word. Re-recorded and re-released, it became a hit. Name that tune.

7. Why was Julie Covington's 1976 UK No.1 'Don't Cry for Me Argentina' later banned?

8. Paul McCartney and Wings' 'Hi, Hi, Hi' was banned for supposed drug references. True or false?

9. Surely no one would ban The Beach Boys' timeless love song 'God Only Knows'? Well, yes they would – but why?

10. The Kingsmen's 'Louie Louie' was a US No.2 in 1963, even though most of the lyrics were indecipherable. So why was it banned?
    a) Someone found the original lyrics and had them published in a national newspaper
    b) Radio stations felt that singer Jack Ely's slurred delivery was designed to hide rude words
    c) There was a national scandal involving Ely at the time

11. **Why did a Texas radio station ban all Bob Dylan's records in 1968?**
a) Because his songs were too political
b) Because of comments he'd made about that radio station
c) Because they couldn't decipher his cryptic lyrics and were
concerned that they might be spreading rude or politically
controversial ideas

12. **Incredibly, 'Ding–Dong! The Witch is Dead', from *The Wizard of Oz* (1939), was banned by the BBC in 2013 – despite climbing to No.2 on the UK charts. It was felt that it might be too closely associated with the recent death of a famous politician. But who?**

13. **In 2018, 'Baby, It's Cold Outside' was banned by a Cleveland radio station. It had been around (unbanned) since 1944, so what prompted the action now?**
a) Some listeners felt the lyrics suggested sexual harassment and
hinted at date rape
b) Some listeners believed they'd found hidden expletives in the lyrics
c) Some listeners detected racist undertones in the lyrics

14. **David Bowie's 1969 hit 'Space Oddity' was banned while the Apollo 11 mission to the Moon was in progress. Why?**
a) The lyrics seemed to contain drug references
b) Because of a controversial TV performance of the song by Bowie
c) The idea of an astronaut getting lost in space seemed in poor taste
while the Moon mission was ongoing

15. **Which Phil Collins song was banned during the First Gulf War?**
a) 'In the Air Tonight'
b) 'I Missed Again'
c) 'Thru' These Walls'

16. **Which of these Sex Pistols songs *wasn't* banned?**
a) 'Anarchy in the UK'
b) 'Friggin' in the Riggin''
c) 'God Save the Queen'

DID YOU KNOW?

In the early 1970s, the children's ditty 'Puff the Magic Dragon' was
banned because of its alleged references to marijuana.

Quiz 4

Court Is in Session

From plagiarism to devilishly concealed messages aimed at credulous fans, artists have spent plenty of time in the dock over the years. So are the following pop trivia chin-scratchers difficult or not difficult? You be the judge.

Answers page 237

1. In 2015, a court ruled that a best-selling (and highly controversial) single co-written by Pharrell Williams had borrowed heavily from Marvin Gaye's 1977 single 'Got to Give It Up'. What was the single?

2. Which rap diva's 'nail rage' incident in 2004 led to a spell in jail?

3. Which charming man was described as 'devious, truculent and unreliable' by a judge in 1996, in a case over royalties not paid to other members of the band?

4. In 1967, *Times* editor William Rees-Mogg wrote an article entitled 'Who breaks a butterfly on a wheel?', protesting at heavy sentences handed down to two musicians on drugs charges. They happened to be in one of the Sixties' most famous bands. Who were they?

5. In 1976, George Harrison was found guilty of plagiarizing (albeit unconsciously) a girl-group hit from the Sixties for his signature best-seller, 'My Sweet Lord'. What was the song he unintentionally borrowed from?
   a) 'He's So Fine', by The Chiffons
   b) 'Be My Baby', by The Ronettes
   c) 'Please Mr. Postman', by The Marvelettes

6. Oasis's songwriter Noel Gallagher has openly borrowed from other people's past musical glories. But one early hit was so clearly similar to 'I'd Like to Teach the World to Sing (In Perfect Harmony)', the backing to a famous early Seventies Coca-Cola commercial, that he was sued and forced to pay out. What was the Oasis song?
   a) 'Live Forever'
   b) 'Shakermaker'
   c) 'Supersonic'

7. The Beach Boys appropriated Chuck Berry's 'Sweet Little Sixteen' for one of their defining early hits. What was it?

8. John Lennon settled out of court with Chuck Berry after he borrowed from the latter's 'You Can't Catch Me' for a 1969 Beatles song. Name that song.

9. Joe Satriani's 'If I Could Fly' bore something of a resemblance to a life-affirming transatlantic No.1 for Coldplay in 2008. So much so that the two settled out of court. Name the Coldplay hit.

10. In 1990, a metal band were taken to court by the parents of two men who had shot themselves. Allegedly, they'd heard subliminal messages urging them to commit suicide in the lyrics of the song 'Better By You, Better Than Me'. Which band?
    a) Guns N' Roses
    b) Slayer
    c) Judas Priest

11. Jello Biafra – lead singer with Californian punk group Dead Kennedys – was put on trial for distributing pornography, prompted by the artwork *Penis Landscape* by H.R. Giger on the band's 1985 *Frankenchrist* album. Was he found guilty or not guilty?

12. In 2012, a band were arrested after performing their anti-establishment 'Punk Prayer' at a Russian Orthodox Church in Moscow. The three were charged with 'hooliganism motivated by religious hatred' and sentenced to two years' imprisonment each. Name the band.

13. Brazilian musician Jorge Ben's track 'Taj Mahal' was a direct inspiration for a colossal disco hit for Rod Stewart. Ben sued, and Stewart immediately owned up, though he insisted he'd done it without realizing. What was the song?

14. Yusuf Islam (formerly Cat Stevens) successfully sued The Flaming Lips because their 2002 'Fight Test' track audibly leant on one of his Seventies classics. But which one?
    a) 'Father and Son'
    b) 'Lady D'Arbanville'
    c) 'Moonshadow'

15. Sex Pistols were forced to go to court after police seized stock in a shop window advertising their debut album *Never Mind the Bollocks, Here's the Sex Pistols* (1977). Which barrister and well-known author (successfully) defended them?
    a) Robert Harris
    b) John le Carré
    c) John Mortimer

Quiz 5

Fashion Killa

Pop's always been as much for the eyes as for
the ears. From profanity-strewn tees and stolen VW
badges to barely-there bras and undead make-up,
we prefer our stars when they're dressed in excess.
But fashionistas beware: 'cool' and 'fool'
hang right next to each other ...

Answers page 238

1. Who rocked up to the 2010 MTV Video Music Awards in a raw beef dress designed by Franc Fernandez?

2. An item of Jean Paul Gaultier lingerie caused a commotion after one star wore it during a 1990 tour. What was it? And who was the star?

3. Who turned up to the Grammys in 2017 in an all-gold outfit (with matching paint for the face) under the pseudonym 'Gnarly Davidson'?

4. Who wore a Vatican-themed red robe, designed by Versace, to the 2012 Grammys?
   a) Nicki Minaj
   b) Lil' Kim
   c) Azealia Banks

5. Russian singer Sasha Gradiva complemented a pink gown with what unusual accessory for the 2012 Grammys?
   a) A chainmail helmet
   b) Machine guns attached to an arm sleeve
   c) A goldfish in its bowl

6. Kurt Cobain wore one onstage. The Lemonheads' Evan Dando was known to as well. David Bowie sported one on an album cover in 1970. What did they wear?

7. Iggy Pop performed on UK music show *The White Room* in 1996. What was unusual about the trousers he was wearing?
   a) The bottom had been cut out
   b) They had been spray-painted on
   c) They were see-through plastic – and he wasn't wearing underwear

8. Who wore a fox head and a red frock onstage, after a character from the front of his band's album *Foxtrot*?

9. Which Seventies glam-rock star once wore a stage outfit (black coat decorated with circular mirrors, topped off with a silver headdress) dubbed 'The Metal Nun' by a fellow band member?

10. At the height of punk, both Sid Vicious and Siouxsie Sioux were criticized for sporting one particularly sensitive symbol. What was it?

11. Who sported a 'flasher's mac', bikini briefs and a neckerchief while touring his 1980 album *Dirty Mind*?

12. Who wore a tutu-like dress with a fake swan neck curled around her neck to the 2001 Academy Awards?

13. Which Rolling Stone posed in a Nazi SS uniform for Danish magazine *Børge* in 1966?

14. Having scored huge hits with the band he'd led, this soul rebel singer's career nosedived when he embraced drag and make-up for the cover of a solo album. His mixed-gender appearance at Reading Festival in 1999 attracted a flurry of bottles from the crowd. Who is he?

15. On which subject, The Rolling Stones controversially donned full drag for the promo film for which of their 1960s singles?

16. At 2012's London Fashion Week, Lady Gaga wore something that attracted criticism of 'cultural thievery' from some quarters. What was it?
a) A full-body burqa
b) A Native American headdress
c) A kimono

DID YOU KNOW?

In 2012, Rihanna arrived at a restaurant in Australia wearing a trench coat. And heels. And, apparently, nothing else.

Quiz 6

My Beautiful Dark Twisted Life

Rapper, producer, genius, egotist and possibly not all there all of the time. Love him or loathe him, there's no one quite like Kanye. And few stars do controversy better. So who better to slam dunk us out of this round than the LeBron of Rhyme?

Answers page 239

1. Kanye infamously burst onstage at different award ceremonies to voice his disagreement about the winners. Name two of the artists whose acceptance speech he's interrupted.

2. Following one of his unscheduled award-crashes, Kanye was criticized as a jackass. By whom?
    a) Hillary Clinton
    b) Barack Obama
    c) Donald Trump

3. Kanye outraged viewers of TMZ Live in 2018 by referring to slavery as ... what?
    a) Overexaggerated
    b) A choice
    c) Inevitable

4. In 2006, Kanye appeared on a *Rolling Stone* cover posing as who?
    a) Muhammad Ali
    b) Malcolm X
    c) Jesus Christ

5. In the lyrics for 'Famous', Kanye contentiously opined that one female star should bed him because he'd made her famous. Who was the woman in question?

6. Kanye designed a sneaker for upmarket fashion brand Louis Vuitton in 2009. During promotion duties, he declared that he was changing his name to – what?
    a) Martin Louis the King Jr
    b) Yeezus Saint Laurent
    c) Juan Pablo de Picasso

7. Kanye has announced that he will run for president in 2020 – true or false?

8. The video for one of his songs featured Kanye in bed alongside a row of nude wax models of celebrities, including Taylor Swift, Rihanna, Donald Trump and Bill Cosby. What was the song?
    a) 'Gold Digger'
    b) 'Champion'
    c) 'Famous'

9.   **What was so controversial about a range of clothing that Kanye began selling in 2013?**
     a) It dissed Barack Obama
     b) It was supportive of the US gun lobby
     c) It featured the Confederate flag

10. **One particular feature of Kanye's Yeezus Tour raised more eyebrows than most. What was it?**
     a) He had a mock crucifixion enacted onstage
     b) He claimed to be able to heal sick people
     c) He had a 'co-star' in the form of an actor dressed as Jesus Christ

11. **Naked models arranged as dead bodies – some headless, a torture scene featuring Nicki Minaj as victim and aggressor, zombies ... no surprise that MTV wanted nothing to do with this video. What's the song?**

12. **In 2016, Kanye tweeted someone to ask them to invest $1 billion in his 'ideas'. Who was his potential benefactor?**

13. **What did Kanye controversially suggest abolishing in 2018?**
     a) The 13th Amendment (which legally ended the practice of slavery in the USA)
     b) Corporate tax
     c) Obamacare

14. **What was it about the lyrics to 'XTCY' that raised eyebrows?**

15. **In 2004, Kanye stormed out of the American Music Awards after he was beaten to a top prize by country singer Gretchen Wilson. He later declared to the press that he had been 'robbed'. What was the award he missed out on?**
     a) Tour of the Year
     b) Best Music Video
     c) New Artist of the Year

ROUND 5

ON RECORD

Quiz 1

Cover to Cover

Music's only part of the package. For decades now,
acts have used the covers of their records (or CDs)
to further express themselves. From Patti Smith to
Lady Gaga, we peruse the LP livery of yesterday and today.

Answers page 240

1. A famous British Pop Artist and his then wife designed the Grammy-winning cover of The Beatles' *Sgt. Pepper's Lonely Hearts Club Band* (1967). Name him and – for an extra point – name her too.

2. Which famous West Coast comix artist drew the cover for Big Brother and the Holding Company's classic 1968 album *Cheap Thrills*?
   a) Robert Crumb
   b) Charles M. Schulz
   c) Charles Addams

3. Who provided the phantasmagorical cover artwork for Yes's albums *Fragile* (1971), *Close to the Edge* (1972) and *Tales from Topographic Oceans* (1973)?

4. The cover shot for Patti Smith's 1975 album *Horses* was taken by a photographer who had once lived with her (as documented in her book *Just Kids*). He would go on to make his name producing highly controversial homoerotic photos. Name him.

5. His work includes the infamous picture sleeve for Sex Pistols' single 'God Save the Queen' (1977) and the cover for their album *Never Mind the Bollocks, Here's the Sex Pistols* from the same year. Who is he?
   a) Andy Warhol
   b) Jamie Reid
   c) H.R. Giger

6. Which Lady Gaga album cover was designed by artist Jeff Koons?
   a) *Born This Way* (2011)
   b) *Artpop* (2013)
   c) *Joanne* (2016)

7. What do the jagged peaks on Joy Division's debut album *Unknown Pleasures* (1979) illustrate?
   a) Radio waves from a pulsar
   b) A series of earthquakes
   c) Heartbeats

8. Which Manic Street Preachers album cover featured a triptych by artist Jenny Saville?

9. Designer Peter Saville created the cover for the best-selling 12-inch single of all time – although it was so expensive to produce that the label actually lost money on every copy sold. Name the band and the song.

10. Which Andy Warhol-designed album cover features the legend 'Peel Slowly and See'?
    a) *The Velvet Underground and Nico* (1967), by The Velvet Underground and Nico
    b) *Sticky Fingers* (1971), by The Rolling Stones
    c) *Love You Live* (1977), by The Rolling Stones

11. The sleeve for Ice Cube's *Death Certificate* (1991) sees the rapper alongside what?
    a) A gravestone with 'Free speech' written on it
    b) A hearse with his double in an open coffin inside
    c) A corpse with a tag reading 'Uncle Sam' on its toe

12. What theme links the sleeves of The Notorious B.I.G.'s *Ready to Die* (1994), Nas's *Illmatic* (1994), Lil Wayne's *Tha Carter III* (2008) and Kendrick Lamar's *Good Kid, M.A.A.D City* (2012)?

13. The cover of Bow Wow Wow's 1982 debut full-length album mimicked a famous 19th-century painting entitled *Le déjeuner sur l'herbe*. Who painted it?

14. Concerning one of his album covers, Bruce Springsteen remembered, 'The picture of my ass looked better than the picture of my face, so that's what went on the cover.' What was the album?

15. The sleeve for Eminem's album *Kamikaze* (2018) pays homage to which Beastie Boys LP?
    a) *Licensed to Ill* (1986)
    b) *Paul's Boutique* (1989)
    c) *Hello Nasty* (1998)

DID YOU KNOW?
The Jimi Hendrix album *Axis: Bold as Love* (1967) was banned in Malaysia after protests from Hindu groups. It portrays the guitarist and his band members as the god Vishnu.

Quiz 2

Wall of Sound

Since the advent of sophisticated recording software, artists have long been able to produce quality sounds 'in the box' with a laptop. But there's still a place for producers to sprinkle a little gold dust on raw talent.

Answers page 241

1. Which of the following Phil Spector productions didn't make
    No.1 in the USA?
    a) 'He's a Rebel', by The Crystals (1962)
    b) 'Be My Baby', by The Ronettes (1963)
    c) 'You've Lost That Lovin' Feelin'', by The Righteous Brothers (1964)

2. He scored a UK No.1 as an artist, then went on to produce hit
    albums for ABC (*The Lexicon of Love*, 1982), Frankie Goes To
    Hollywood (*Welcome to the Pleasuredome*, 1984) and Yes (*90125*,
    1983), as well as Band Aid's 'Do They Know It's Christmas?'
    (1984). Name him.

3. Who produced Nirvana's *Nevermind* (1991)?
    a) Butch Vig
    b) Steve Albini
    c) Trent Reznor

4. One British singer-songwriter won multiple Grammys
    (including Best Record of the Year and Best New Artist)
    for a 2007 album produced by Mark Ronson. Who was it?

5. In 2004, Danger Mouse produced a mash-up of Jay-Z's
    The Black Album (2003) and The Beatles' 'The White Album'
    (1968). What was its title?

6. Elvis Presley, Jerry Lee Lewis and Johnny Cash all began their
    careers with Memphis's Sun Records. Who was the owner
    (and in-house producer) there?

7. Which definitive punk album did Chris Thomas produce?

8. Once named the most important producer of the 1980s by *Rolling
    Stone*, he worked on U2's *The Joshua Tree* (1987), as well as Bob
    Dylan's career-reviving *Time Out of Mind* (1997). Who is he?

9. Which former glam-rock star brought his production skills to
    bear on David Bowie's so-called 'Berlin Trilogy' (*Low*, *"Heroes"*
    and *Lodger*) in the 1970s?

10. 'A true articulation of the anxiety of late 20th-century man backed with music not only of extraordinary grace and melody, but also of experimental clarity and vision.' Which Nigel Godrich-produced 1997 album were *NME* raving about?

11. His recording 'Chicken Scratch', released in the early 1960s, gave this eccentric producer his nickname. Who is he?

12. A chronic-le of success: having contributed to one of the most controversial hip hop albums of the 1980s, he contributed to the production of platinum-selling releases such as Snoop Dogg's *Doggystyle* (1993), Eminem's *The Slim Shady LP* (1999) and 50 Cent's *Get Rich or Die Tryin'* (2003). Name him.

13. Who did MTV dub 'the most important producer of the last 20 years' in 2007?
    a) Mark Ronson
    b) Timbaland
    c) Rick Rubin

14. Who produced the best-selling album of all time?
    a) George Martin
    b) Kanye West
    c) Quincy Jones

15. Which maverick British producer had UK No.1s with 'Telstar', 'Have I the Right?' and 'Johnny Remember Me' in the 1960s?

16. What was the last Beatles album produced by George Martin?
    a) *The Beatles* (aka 'The White Album') (1968)
    b) *Abbey Road* (1969)
    c) *Let It Be* (1970)

Who Sampled Whom?

Back in the day, hip hop artists revolutionized music-making through sampling. It opened up whole new vistas – and, in time, invited lawsuits from the original artists. Let's go crate-digging!

Answers page 242

1. Which song and artist did The Verve's 1997 'Bitter Sweet Symphony' sample, much to their cost?

2. Which Led Zeppelin song was sampled for Björk's 'Army of Me' and Beastie Boys' 'Rhymin' & Stealin'', among others?

3. Which Kanye West track sampled Daft Punk's 'Harder, Better, Faster ...'?

4. Lauryn Hill's 'Ex-Factor' was sampled by Drake for which US No.1 single in 2018?

5. Labi Siffre's 1975 tune 'I Got The ...' re-emerged as a sample on which defining Eminem track in 1999?

6. Sixties vocal group The Turtles successfully sued De La Soul for sampling 'You Showed Me' for 'Transmitting Live from Mars'. On which 1989 album did the latter appear?

7. A British group's sole UK No.1, from 1985, was sampled for Flo Rida feat. Ke$ha's 'Right Round'. Name the original track.

8. Lady Gaga's 'Poker Face' (2009) sampled a 1977 Boney M gangster tune. Name it.

9. In 2008, Hilary Duff had a hit with 'Reach Out', which sampled a classic Depeche Mode hit from 1989. Name it.

10. One of the best-known samples ever is an instrumental break from a James Brown song. Hundreds of songs have sampled it, including 'Party' by Beyoncé and Miley Cyrus's 'We Can't Stop'. What was the original?

11. According to whosampled.com, the most sampled track of all time is 'Amen, Brother' (1969), by The Winstons. But how many times has it been sampled?
a) Around 1,000
b) Around 2,000
c) Around 3,000

12. 'Rapper's Delight' (1979) by The Sugarhill Gang samples Chic's 'Le Freak' (1978). True or false?

13. Sugababes' 'Freak Like Me' (2002) sampled which 1970s synth-pop classic?

14. Soho's 'Hippychick' (1990) appropriated the riff from which Smiths song?
    a) 'How Soon Is Now?' (1984)
    b) 'This Charming Man' (1983)
    c) 'Bigmouth Strikes Again' (1986)

15. Rick James's 'Super Freak' was appropriated by MC Hammer in 1990 – for what track?

16. Kanye West had to write a letter to the composers of 'Kid Charlemagne' to get permission to use a sample from it on 'Champion'. Which band originally recorded the song? And if you know that, you'll probably be able to name the composers too ...
    a) The Doobie Brothers
    b) Steely Dan
    c) The Eagles

Quiz 4

Bringing It All Back Home

To end this round, welcome to a catch-all quiz with a particular emphasis on segassem neddih.

Answers page 243

1. Radiohead's *Kid A* (2000) had a secret booklet hidden behind the back tray of the CD. It featured drawings and what appeared to be random text. But the text wasn't random at all – what was it?
    a) Snippets from Thom Yorke's unpublished autobiography
    b) Lines taken from each band member's favourite novel at the time
    c) Lyrics from the band's next two albums, *Amnesiac* (2001) and *Hail to the Thief* (2003)

2. Missy Elliott's 'Work It' employed a highly original euphemism for the male genitalia. What was it?

3. Unless a stylus automatically rises from a record when it is finished, it will carry on playing in the vinyl's inner groove. On one of Pink Floyd's albums – which did more than just graze the charts – this groove features the sound of an endlessly dripping tap. Name the album.
    a) *The Dark Side of the Moon* (1973)
    b) *Wish You Were Here* (1975)
    c) *Atom Heart Mother* (1970)

4. Which was the first rock album to feature lyrics printed on the cover?

5. Led Zeppelin's album *In Through the Out Door* (1978) came with a hidden treat for fans. What happened if you applied water to the inner sleeve?
    a) The black-and-white illustrations changed to colour
    b) A message appeared, thanking you for buying the album
    c) The picture changed to reveal the faces of the four members of the band

6. Public Enemy's *Muse Sick-n-Hour Mess Age* (1994) included a vitriolic secret track that took on the band's critics. How was it concealed on the album?
    a) It was sped up to five times its original speed, so the words were barely audible
    b) It played only after a gap of 30 minutes following the final listed track on the album
    c) It was hidden in the pre-gap before the CD started

7. What do you see when you hold up the inner gatefold sleeve of David Bowie's *Blackstar* (2015) to sunlight?

8. The aeroplane on the cover of Beastie Boys' *Licensed to Ill* (1986) features the serial number '3MTA3'. What does it signify?

9. Monty Python's album *Matching Tie and Handkerchief* (1973) actually featured three sides. How so?
    a) There was a double groove on one side of the original vinyl LP, each one featuring different tracks. Whichever one the stylus landed in would play
    b) There was a flexi-disc album included as part of the cover
    c) They gave away another, one-sided vinyl album along with it at purchase

10. ELO's 'Mr. Blue Sky' (1978) ends with a vocoded voice telling the listener to 'Please turn me over'. Why that message?

11. Which Nirvana album was provisionally titled *I Hate Myself and I Want to Die*?

12. What was notable about Lauryn Hill's cover of 'Can't Take My Eyes Off You', a hidden track on her album *The Miseducation of Lauryn Hill* (1999)?
    a) It was nominated for a Best Female Pop Vocal Grammy
    b) Lauryn Hill didn't know it had been added to the album
    c) It was sung in Spanish

13. The 'ultra' edition of one Jack White album included a trove of hidden treasures, including secret tracks running at 33rpm and 78rpm, tracks under the record labels and a reverse groove on side one (so the record plays from its centre to its outer edge). So: what's the album?
    a) *Blunderbuss* (2012)
    b) *Lazaretto* (2014)
    c) *Boarding House Reach* (2018)

14. In 1997, one hot alternative-rock band produced an album in the form of four CDs that had to be played simultaneously. Who are they? And for the kiss-off, name the album.

15. Wu-Tang Clan's *Once Upon a Time in Shaolin* (2015) is unique – in what respect?

ICONIC
ARTISTS

Quiz 1

Elvis Presley

Which Elvis is your favourite? The Fifties firebrand? The God-fearing gospel singer? The jumpsuited balladeer? While you're pondering that, ponder this ...

Answers page 244

1. Elvis's best-selling single (20 million copies plus) was based on the Neapolitan song ''O sole mio'. By what name is it better known?

2. By what name is Andreas Cornelis van Kuijk better known?

3. Which was Elvis's favourite of his own films?
    a) *King Creole* (1958)
    b) *G.I. Blues* (1960)
    c) *Blue Hawaii* (1961)

4. What was Elvis's first *Billboard* No.1? And for a bonus point, what was his last?

5. In 1953, Big Mama Thornton topped the US R&B charts with a high-class song written by Jerry Leiber and Mike Stoller. In 1956, Elvis took it to No.1 on the *Billboard* Hot 100. What was the song?

6. His pelvic thrusts saw Elvis censored by one US TV show, which famously only showed him from the waist up in 1957. What was the programme?
    a) *The Milton Berle Show*
    b) *The Steve Allen Show*
    c) *The Ed Sullivan Show*

7. Who did Elvis welcome to his Hollywood home on 27 August 1965?
    a) The Beatles
    b) The Rolling Stones
    c) Bob Dylan

8. What was Elvis's first movie?
    a) *Love Me Tender*
    b) *Jailhouse Rock*
    c) *Flaming Star*

9. What is Elvis's best-selling album?
    a) *Elvis' Christmas Album* (1957)
    b) *Elvis Is Back!* (1960)
    c) *Blue Hawaii* soundtrack (1961)

10. What iconic item of fashion did Nudie Cohn create for Elvis in 1957?

11. **In the 1970s, the acronym 'TCB' became associated with Elvis, providing the name of his backing band and also featuring on personal gifts he handed out. It represented a personal motto for the King – but what did it stand for?**
a) Truth Can't be Beat
b) This Can be Better
c) Taking Care of Business

12. **Almost eight years after his last live appearance, Elvis returned to the stage in 1969 – but where?**
a) Madison Square Garden in New York
b) The Hollywood Bowl in Los Angeles
c) The International Hotel in Las Vegas

13. **Which Country & Western star wrote 'Always on My Mind', which Elvis charted with in 1972?**
a) Dolly Parton
b) Waylon Jennings
c) Willie Nelson

14. **How many Grammys did Elvis win?**
a) Three
b) Nine
c) Twelve

15. **What significant event in Elvis's life took place on 26 June 1977?**
a) He was officially divorced from his wife, Priscilla
b) He played his last concert
c) He finished recording his last album

16. **On 30 April 1976, a rising rock star scaled the walls outside Elvis's home, Graceland – although he was stopped before he could get inside. Who was he?**
a) Gene Simmons
b) David Bowie
c) Bruce Springsteen

Quiz 2

The Beatles

Pop in 1962 and pop in 1970 were worlds apart. Much of that is down to the Fabs, whose career was a magical mystery tour from seedy Hamburg bars to Shea Stadium, 'Love Me Do' to 'Strawberry Fields Forever', broke rockers to hippie millionaires. But just how well do you know the world's most famous band?

Answers page 245

1. Stuart Sutcliffe, the 'Fifth Beatle', left the group in 1961 to pursue his artistic career. He studied at the Hamburg College of Art under a well-known British Pop Artist. Was it ...
a) Peter Blake
b) David Hockney
c) Eduardo Paolozzi

2. What was the best-selling Beatles single in the UK?

3. The sole John Lennon/George Harrison Beatles composition was an instrumental. Name it.
a) 'Thinking of Linking'
b) 'Cry for a Shadow'
c) 'Take My Baby Home'

4. Which Beatles album was the first (and only) one to feature solely Lennon/McCartney songs?

5. What is the longest Beatles track? And for a bonus point, what is the shortest one?

6. Before joining The Beatles, which Liverpool band did Ringo Starr drum with?
a) Rory Storm and the Hurricanes
b) Gerry and the Pacemakers
c) The Swinging Blue Jeans

7. Who was the first Beatle to release a solo album? And for a bonus point, what was it?

8. What was the first Lennon/McCartney song to reach No.1 for another artist?
a) 'Step Inside Love' by Cilla Black
b) 'A World Without Love', by Peter and Gordon
c) 'Bad to Me', by Billy J. Kramer and the Dakotas

9. What was George Harrison's first solo Beatles composition?
a) 'Something'
b) 'Here Comes the Sun'
c) 'Don't Bother Me'

10. **When did John Lennon return his MBE?**
    a) 1969
    b) 1973
    c) 1977

11. **What did Paul McCartney write 'Got to Get You into My Life' about?**
    a) LSD
    b) Transcendental Meditation
    c) Marijuana

12. **The Beatles' debut appearance on *The Ed Sullivan Show* in February 1964 drew a huge TV audience in the States. How many viewers tuned in?**
    a) 23 million
    b) 53 million
    c) 73 million

13. **The so-called 'butcher sleeve' was an infamous 1966 album cover depicting the Fabs in butcher's smocks, clutching joints of meat and dismembered dolls. What was the album's actual title?**
    a) *A Collection of Beatles Oldies (But Goldies!)*
    b) *The Beatles ... So Far*
    c) *Yesterday and Today*

14. **What was the first Beatles single released on their own Apple label?**

15. **'With a Little Help from My Friends' has been a UK No.1 three times, although never for The Beatles themselves. Name any one of the chart-toppers.**

16. **As well as The Beatles, which other musician is credited on the single 'Get Back'?**

> **SAY WHAT?**
> 'Even I can't keep up with our own image. I come into Apple one day, and there's George got a new head on him.' John Lennon (*NME*, 3 May 1969)

Quiz 3

The Rolling Stones

Scruffier and more threatening than The Beatles, the Stones had their own formidable writing team in Mick Jagger and Keith Richards. Riotous gigs and a string of timeless singles established their legend in the Sixties, while the Seventies saw them become 'The Greatest Rock'n'Roll Band in the World', a title they're still defending today.

Answers page 246

1. The group was named (by guitarist Brian Jones) after a song by which blues performer?

2. Which one of the original six-piece Rolling Stones was sacked because he didn't fit in with the group's image?

3. What was the first Jagger/Richards UK No.1 for the Stones?

4. And what was the band's last US No.1 to date?

5. Who recorded the original version of 'Not Fade Away', which the Stones took to No.3 in the UK in early 1964?

6. On which Stones No.1 does Brian Jones play a sitar?

7. When they performed on *The Ed Sullivan Show* in 1967, the band were forced to re-word the chorus of their current single 'Let's Spend the Night Together'. To what?
    a) 'Take Time to Be Together'
    b) 'Let's Try to Get Together'
    c) 'Let's Spend Some Time Together'

8. In which London green space did The Rolling Stones give a free concert in 1969?
    a) Hyde Park
    b) Richmond Park
    c) Regent's Park

9. Which cult movie starred Mick Jagger opposite James Fox (and also featured Keith Richards's then girlfriend, Anita Pallenberg)?

10. The band became tax exiles in 1971. To which country did they move?
    a) Germany
    b) France
    c) Spain

11. Which Stone wrote the children's book *Ode to a High Flying Bird*, a tribute to Charlie Parker?

12. Ronnie Wood replaced Mick Taylor as the Stones' guitarist in 1975. What was Wood's former band?

13. Who officially left the band in 1993?

14. Which renowned film-maker directed the Stones' in-concert movie *Shine a Light* (2008)?
     a) Francis Ford Coppola
     b) Martin Scorsese
     c) Jim Jarmusch

15. What was the title of Keith Richards's acclaimed 2010 autobiography?

16. The band's 2016 release *Blue & Lonesome* was the first of their LPs to consist entirely of cover versions. True or false?

Quiz 4

Sex Pistols

They were pilloried in the mainstream press, their gigs and records were banned and they were attacked in the streets. Hard to believe now that one band could have seemed so dangerous. But with an incendiary musical attack topped off by a voice – and lyrics – shockingly new, Sex Pistols' impact went far beyond the charts. Never mind the bollocks ... here's the quiz.

Answers page 247

1. **The first documented Sex Pistols gig took place in London in November 1975 – where?**
    a) The Marquee
    b) The 100 Club
    c) Saint Martin's School of Art

2. **According to legend, which Alice Cooper song did John Lydon sing along to for his 'audition' with the band?**
    a) 'School's Out'
    b) 'I'm Eighteen'
    c) 'Elected'

3. **In 1973, Steve Jones stole some equipment after a concert in Hammersmith, London, by which famous act?**
    a) David Bowie
    b) Marc Bolan
    c) Roxy Music

4. **The band's gig at Manchester's Lesser Free Trade Hall in 1976 was arranged by two future members of Buzzcocks. Name them.**

5. **The Pistols appeared on the *Today* chat show in December 1976, and outraged viewers (and the press) by swearing live on air. They'd actually been invited on as a substitute for another killer band – who?**

6. **ABBA's 'SOS' inspired the riff for a Sex Pistols song. Which one?**
    a) 'Anarchy in the UK'
    b) 'Holidays in the Sun'
    c) 'Pretty Vacant'

7. **The band 'signed' to A&M Records during a staged event for the press in March 1977 (although the actual signing had taken place days before). Outside which famous site did the ceremony take place?**
    a) New Scotland Yard
    b) The Houses of Parliament
    c) Buckingham Palace

8. **Which label did Sex Pistols sign with after they were dropped by A&M Records in May 1977?**

9. Despite a blanket radio ban, the band's single 'God Save the Queen' reached No.2 on the UK charts. It was held off the top spot by which Rod Stewart song?
   a) 'Maggie May'
   b) 'The First Cut Is the Deepest'/'I Don't Want to Talk About It'
   c) 'Da Ya Think I'm Sexy?'

10. The Pistols played their final UK gig in Huddersfield during Christmas 1977. But on which day?
    a) Christmas Eve
    b) Christmas Day
    c) Boxing Day

11. In which city did the band play their last gig before splitting up?
    a) New York
    b) Los Angeles
    c) San Francisco

12. After the Pistols split, Sid Vicious and girlfriend Nancy Spungen lived in which famous bohemian New York hangout?

13. Which ex-Pistol went on to form Rich Kids?

14. What was the name of the Sex Pistols movie released in 1980?

15. Match the autobiography to the ex-Pistol:
    a) John Lydon   1) *Lonely Boy: Tales from a Sex Pistol*
    b) Steve Jones   2) *I Was a Teenage Sex Pistol*
    c) Glen Matlock   3) *Anger Is an Energy: My Life Uncensored*

16. In what year did the band re-form for the Filthy Lucre Tour?
    a) 1994
    b) 1996
    c) 1998

DID YOU KNOW?
The Sex Pistols were sacked from A&M Records just 10 days after signing.

Quiz 5

Madonna

She transformed music in the Eighties with a host
of infectious singles, an appetite for reinvention and
a penchant for stirring up controversy. Her stage
shows became bigger and raunchier as her profile
rocketed, but she always retained her pop nous.
All hail, Her Madge!

Answers page 248

1. Before becoming a solo artist, Madonna was in a rock band
    with the same name as an Eighties brat-pack movie. What was
    it called?
    a) The Outsiders
    b) The Breakfast Club
    c) Pretty in Pink

2. What was her role in the band?
    a) Drummer
    b) Bassist
    c) Backing vocalist

3. What was her first *Billboard* Hot 100 No.1?

4. Who did she star opposite in *Desperately Seeking Susan* (1985)?

5. The video for her single 'Material Girl' paid homage to
    'Diamonds Are a Girl's Best Friend' from *Gentlemen Prefer
    Blondes* (1953). Who performed it in that film?

6. Madonna's The Virgin Tour took place in North America
    in 1985. Who was her support act?
    a) The Police
    b) Level 42
    c) Beastie Boys

7. What is Madonna's best-selling album?

8. In 1989, Pepsi ended its sponsorship deal with Madonna after
    an outcry over her latest video – for which song?

9. What character did she play in the movie *Dick Tracy* (1990)?

10. Which film secured Madonna her first Golden Globe?

11. Which rock star was a co-writer on 'Justify My Love'?
    a) Bruce Springsteen
    b) Lenny Kravitz
    c) Prince

12. **Which was the first of her songs to debut at No.1 in the UK?**
    a) 'Ray of Light'
    b) 'Frozen'
    c) 'American Pie'

13. **For which movie did she sing 'Beautiful Stranger'?**

14. **Madonna provoked controversy at the 2003 MTV Music Video Awards by kissing her two female co-performers while singing 'Hollywood'. Who were they?**

15. **She holds the record for the highest-grossing tour by a solo artist. But which tour was it?**
    a) Blond Ambition World Tour
    b) Drowned World Tour
    c) Sticky & Sweet Tour

16. **She has a star on Hollywood's Walk of Fame. True or false?**

DID YOU KNOW?
Madonna has never had a million-selling single in the UK.

Quiz 6

Prince

During his imperial phase, Prince Rogers Nelson could do no wrong, effortlessly gliding between funk, stadium rock, psychedelic pop and tear-jerking ballads with a click of his high heels. Add his wild productivity, singular battiness and penchant for head-turning outfits, and he just might have been the perfect pop star.

Answers page 249

1. What was the title of Prince's debut album?
   a) *Prince*
   b) *Controversy*
   c) *For You*

2. In 1987, Prince abruptly shelved a funk-influenced album, reportedly because he had a spiritual epiphany and became convinced that it was 'evil'. It went on to become one of the most coveted bootleg LPs of all time, before its commercial release in 1994. Name it.

3. What was the name of Prince's backing band on his mega-selling *Purple Rain* album?

4. ... and who were his final backing band, heard on 2014's *Plectrumelectrum* album?

5. What was Prince's first *Billboard* Hot 100 No.1?

6. In 1986, Prince recorded an album under a feminine pseudonym, although the record was never released. Name that female alter ego.

7. *Crystal Ball* was planned as a triple LP but was eventually released – pared down – under another title. What was it?

8. Prince's recording studio shared its name both with a record label he set up and a track on 1985's *Around the World in a Day* album. Name it.

9. By what name is Prince's archive – reputed to contain thousands of unreleased tracks – known?

10. In August and September 2007, Prince played a run of 21 gigs in London to a combined audience of 350,000. What was the venue?

11. When George Harrison was posthumously inducted into the Rock and Roll Hall of Fame in 2004, Prince stole the show with a ferocious guitar solo during one of the ex-Beatle's best-known songs. What was it?

12. Set in the 1930s, Prince's second movie bombed with critics and public alike. What was its title?

13. In 2017, Pantone announced that it would create a bespoke hue in honour of Prince, dubbed 'Love Symbol No.2'. What colour was it?
    a) Peach
    b) Purple
    c) Gold

14. In 1986, Prince brought the band Mazarati to his studio and offered them a new song. Ecstatic at the results, he wound up releasing it himself – and scoring his third US No.1. Name that tune.

15. Which religious denomination did Prince join in 2001?

16. In July 1984, Prince achieved a notable trilogy of No.1s. What were they?

SAY WHAT?

'In the Eighties, I was out on the road in a massive downward spiral with drink and drugs, I saw *Purple Rain* in a cinema in Canada, I had no idea who he was, it was like a bolt of lightning! ... In the middle of my depression, and the dreadful state of the music culture at that time, it gave me hope, he was like a light in the darkness.' Eric Clapton (Facebook, 23 April 2016)

Quiz 7

Nirvana

They were unlikely stars, a punk-metal band with a candy-pop sensibility who seemed destined for cult status only. In Kurt Cobain, however, they had a songwriter of rare talent and an utterly original vocalist. It couldn't last – Cobain's insecurities would see to that – but in five short years, from their debut album to his death – they turned rock around.

Answers page 250

1. Who did Dave Grohl replace when he became Nirvana's drummer?

2. Which of the following labels were Nirvana *not* on?
   a) Sub Pop
   b) DGC (David Geffen Company)
   c) CBS

3. 'Smells Like Teen Spirit' was Nirvana's first *Billboard* Hot 100 No.1 single. True or false?

4. For their *MTV Unplugged in New York* performance, the band played a track from their debut LP. Name it.

5. Lori Goldston joined the band for their 1993–94 tour and *MTV Unplugged in New York*. What did she play?

6. Which Nirvana album entered the *Billboard* 200 charts at No.1?

7. Nirvana's debut single 'Love Buzz' was a cover version. Which band originally released it?
   a) Blue Mink
   b) Shocking Blue
   c) Blues Magoos

8. Aside from 'Smells Like Teen Spirit', name two of the other single releases from *Nevermind*.

9. What's the name of the 'secret' track on later editions of the CD of *Nevermind* (1992)?

10. Krist Novoselic isn't just a bassist. Name one keyboard instrument he also plays.

11. Name two of the artists Nirvana covered for *MTV Unplugged in New York*.

12. At the MTV Video Music Awards in 1992, the band were forbidden to play one of their songs. Which one?

13. What is 'Teen Spirit'?
    a) A shampoo
    b) A body wash
    c) A deodorant

14. In what year did Kurt marry Courtney Love?
    a) 1991
    b) 1992
    c) 1993

15. How many records have Nirvana sold worldwide to date?
    a) 25 million
    b) 50 million
    c) 75 million

16. Dave Grohl formed Foo Fighters after Nirvana folded. What was their debut single?

SAY WHAT?

'*Nevermind* is a very safe record. It's not like Big Black or the Butthole Surfers, something totally left of centre. We're just slightly left of centre. It's pop. It's just that the guitars are heavy.'
Krist Novoselic (*NME*, 21 March 1992)

Quiz 8

Beyoncé

Success with Destiny's Child was just the start.
Queen Bey's star has risen relentlessly since
then as she ramps up expectations with each
new release, stage show or video. Think you're
crazy in love with her? Then take the test ...

Answers page 251

1. What is Beyoncé's middle name?

2. What was the biggest US hit single for Destiny's Child?

3. What's her best-selling album to date?

4. From 2000 to 2009 she was the best-selling artist in the USA. True or false?

5. She is the only artist to have debuted at No.1 on the *Billboard* Hot 200 with her first six solo albums. What was the sixth?

6. Which Beyoncé No.1 single samples The Chi-Lites' 'Are You My Woman? (Tell Me So)'?

7. What character did Beyoncé play in *Austin Powers in Goldmember* (2002)?
    a) Bébé Fox
    b) Roxette Foxette
    c) Foxxy Cleopatra

8. Beyoncé's second solo album, *B'Day*, came out on 4 September 2006. What is significant about the date?

9. Which trio were the girl group in the movie *Dreamgirls* (2006) based on?

10. Beyoncé's third album introduced (and was named after) her alter ego. What is her name?

11. When Kanye West interrupted Taylor Swift's acceptance speech at the 2009 MTV Video Music Awards, he complained that Beyoncé should have won. Which song's video did he think should have picked up the award?

12. What's the name of Beyoncé's fashion line?
    a) House of Deréon
    b) House of Bey
    c) House of Soul

13.   In the video for which song does Bey take a baseball bat to a series of cars and a fire hydrant, among other things?

14.   She guests on the single (and in the video) for the song 'Telephone' – by whom?

15.   In which streaming service is she a stakeholder?
      a) Spotify
      b) Apple Music
      c) Tidal

16.   *Everything Is Love* (2018) is a joint studio album by Beyoncé and ... who?

DID YOU KNOW?

Beyoncé is the first female artist in history to top the US and UK singles and albums charts simultaneously. She did it in 2003 with 'Crazy in Love' and *Dangerously in Love*.

DON'T FEAR
THE REAPER

Quiz 1

I'll Never Get Out of This World Alive

Those wishing to see out their full three score years and ten might do well to avoid rock'n'roll. For every Jerry Lee Lewis (84 and going strong, as we go to press) there's a Sid Vicious, Kurt Cobain or Janis Joplin …

Answers page 252

1. Just before Christmas 1964, one of soul music's most sublime singers was silenced when he was shot by a motel manager who later claimed he had attacked her. Who was he?

2. Almost three years later to the day, another soul legend drowned when the plane carrying him and his band crashed into the icy waters of Wisconsin's Lake Monona. R.E.S.P.E.C.T. Who was he?

3. Which Sixties guitarist drowned in 1969 in the grounds of a house that had once belonged to Winnie the Pooh creator A.A. Milne?

4. What was the last Doors album Jim Morrison recorded before his death?
   a) *The Soft Parade*
   b) *L.A. Woman*
   c) *Morrison Hotel*

5. This former member of The Byrds overdosed in the Joshua Tree Inn, California, in 1973. Bizarrely, his body was then hijacked by two of his friends, who took it out into Joshua Tree monument and – in response to a prior pact – drenched it in gasoline and set fire to it. His headstone reads 'God's Own Singer'. Name him.

6. Marc Bolan once prophetically told his manager, Simon Napier-Bell, 'I think I'd like to die in a car crash just like [James] Dean, only I'm so small it would have to be a ——'. What kind of car did the elfin star have in mind?

7. Cass Elliot of The Mamas and the Papas died in an apartment in Mayfair, London, in 1974. Four years later, a wild man of rock accidentally overdosed there too. Who?

8. Which electrifying hard-rock singer was found dead in a car in East Dulwich, London, in February 1980?

9. Guitarist Randy Rhoads perished when the pilot of a plane he was flying in 'buzzed' the tour bus too low and crashed into a nearby house. Which noirish singer was he touring with at the time?

10. In 1987, thieves shot and killed the singer who'd been one-third of reggae royalty The Wailers. Name him.

11. His 1994 suicide note quoted a Neil Young lyric; Young, in turn, wrote 'Sleeps with Angels' for him. Name the late legend.

12. Drive-by shootings ended the lives of two A-list rappers in 1996 and 1997 respectively. Name either of them.

13. He walked into the Mississippi on 29 May 1997; not long after, his body re-emerged at the foot of Beale Street, Memphis's home of the blues. Cue hallelujahs to his talent. Who was he?

14. Well versed in excessive behaviour, this singer was found hanged, naked, from a door. The verdict was suicide, though he was no blond. Name him.

15. In 2002, Lisa 'Left Eye' Lopes died in a car crash. Of which chart-topping trio was she a member?

16. Abandoning the life of small-time crime and raising hell, this revered musician was part of the group who scored hip hop's first platinum-selling album. He was shot point-blank in his studio in 2002. Who was he?
a) Jam Master Jay
b) DJ Screw
c) Eazy-E

DID YOU KNOW?
As far as we know, Mike Edwards's demise is unique in the annals of rock'n'roll. The ELO cellist was killed in September 2010 when a hay bale rolled down a hillside and hit his van.

Quiz 2

Someone Saved My Life Tonight

Sometimes, the bullet with your name on it misses. Don't ask us why, but every now and then the Angel of Death opts to put his scythe back on the hatstand rather than mow down another singer before they get old. So here's to the reaper cheaters ...

Answers page 253

1. Waylon Jennings gave up his plane seat to a poorly fellow musician in the winter of 1959. That decision saved his life. Name any of the three musicians who died when the same plane crashed soon afterwards.

2. One modish singer almost met his personal Jesus in 1996 when he shot up a huge speedball, overdosed and was clinically dead for two minutes – during which (he later claimed) his soul floated up and looked down on his body. Who is he?

3. Mötley Crüe liked to party. But one of them nearly took it too far in 1987 by overdosing on heroin and turning blue, then dying – *dying!* – before being revived by paramedics, discharging himself from hospital, re-recording his home answerphone message to say 'I'm not at home because I'm dead', then shooting up and passing out again. So who had more lives than a cat?
    a) Nikki Sixx
    b) Tommy Lee
    c) Vince Neil

4. After years of drinking and popping pills, this killer performer's stomach ruptured in 1981. He survived and is still with us today – a fact that leaves us slightly breathless. Who is he?

5. He's survived having his dope laced with strychnine, suffered an onstage electrocution and fell asleep with a lit cigarette, setting his bed on fire. His house burned down too, although he blamed that on a mouse chewing through wires. After nuclear Armageddon, so the joke goes, there'll only be two things left: cockroaches and ————. Name the lucky rocker.

6. Talk about an appetite for (self-)destruction. Which member of Guns N' Roses swallowed his entire stash before going through customs, leading to him spending 96 hours in a coma?
    a) Slash
    b) Izzy Stradlin
    c) Matt Sorum

7. In December 1988, he and his wife were due to catch PAN AM Flight 103 but she couldn't finish packing in time. They missed their flight but kept their lives: the plane blew up over the Scottish town of Lockerbie. Name him.

8. After years of working through a truckload of drugs and booze, the nearest he came to dying was in 2003, when his all-terrain vehicle (ATV) flipped over while he was driving it. Who is he?

9. This Queen had a near-death experience on the operating table in 2012 during leg surgery, but recovered. Now everything runs like clockwork again. Who is he?

10. This GNR booze hound had his wake-up call in 1994: after years of abuse, his pancreas ruptured, giving him third-degree burns. One more drink, he was assured, would kill him. Who is he?
   a) Axl Rose
   b) Slash
   c) Duff McKagan

11. After being shot nine times, you'd think you'd gotta make it to heaven. But this rapper clearly wasn't supposed to die that night. Name him.

12. This rapper was hell-bound in 1996 after taking an overdose of Tylenol when his girlfriend left him and stopped him from seeing his daughter. Fortunately, he failed to die. His name is ...?

13. A friend once found him with his head in a gas oven, distraught at being engaged to a woman when he knew he was gay. He got through it, and his career took off like a rocket, man! Someone saved his life that night – but who is he?

14. Personal traumas saw this disco diva attempt to end it all in 1976 by jumping from a hotel window. Her foot got caught, and at that moment the maid arrived, causing her to come to her senses. Name her.

DID YOU KNOW?
Metallica's James Hetfield was nearly a goner in 1992 when an onstage exploding pyrotechnic set fire to him. Despite second- and third-degree burns, he lived to rock out another day. Ironically, the song the band were playing at the time was 'Fade to Black'.

Quiz 3

Dead Man's Curve

Since the 1950s, teen tragedies and deathbed farewells have peppered the upper reaches of the charts. Test yourself on the history of this maudlin œuvre – but don't expect a happy ending ...

Answers page 254

1. **'Black Denim Trousers and Motorcycle Boots' – the classic
   death-disc outfit – was the first *Billboard* Top 10 hit in 1955 for
   a songwriting duo who were writing for Elvis Presley
   the following year. Who were they?**
   a) Gerry Goffin and Carole King
   b) Doc Pomus and Mort Shuman
   c) Jerry Leiber and Mike Stoller

2. **Mark Dinning's 'Teen Angel' (1959) tells the sorry tale of
   a teenager who runs to retrieve a treasured object from a car
   stalled on train tracks ... What was it that she'd wanted?**
   a) Her boyfriend's photograph
   b) Her boyfriend's sweater
   c) Her boyfriend's class ring

3. **What happens to the doomed teen lovers in Johnny Preston's
   'Running Bear' (1959)?**
   a) They join hands and jump off a cliff
   b) They walk into the desert and are never seen again
   c) They drown

4. **How did the subject of 1960 UK No.1 'Tell Laura I Love Her'
   perish?**

5. **What was the name of John Leyton's 1961 British No.1 about
   a young man haunted by the voice of his deceased girlfriend?**

6. **Schoolgirl Brenda Spencer's shooting spree inspired which 1979 hit?**

7. **Who produced The Shangri-Las' 1964 biker death ditty
   'Leader of the Pack'?**
   a) Phil Spector
   b) Joe Meek
   c) George 'Shadow' Morton

8. **Morrissey-approved singer Twinkle had a British hit in
   1964 with another tale of a spurned boyfriend and a crashed
   motorbike. Name it.**

9.   Surf-rock duo Jan and Dean had a *Billboard* Top 10 hit in 1964 with a song about a fatal car crash at a Los Angeles black spot. Eerily, two years later Dean had a serious automobile accident near a spot with the same name as their hit. What was the song?

10. 'Ode to Billie Joe' – the story of a teenager who leaps to his death from a bridge – was a transatlantic No.1 in 1967. Who was the singer?

11. Jacques Brel's 'Le Moribond' ('The Dying Man') was the inspiration for which 1974 UK chart-topper?

12. Hot Chocolate had an atypical 1974 UK No.3 hit with a downbeat elegy for a failed actress who commits suicide. What was it?

13. The death of a young fan in a car accident on the way to a Kiss show inspired one of the band's signature songs in 1976. Name it.

14. Paul Evans had a *Billboard* Top 10 hit in 1959 with 'Seven Little Girls Sitting in the Backseat'. In 1978, he had an altogether less cheery hit about a grieving boyfriend listening to his late girlfriend's voice on her answerphone. Name it.

15. Prince died precisely 31 years to the day after recording a song about the death of a character in one of his movies. Name the song.

16. On which Eminem song does a neurotic fan meet a watery demise?

> **DID YOU KNOW?**
> 'Death discs' didn't go unmocked. Period parodies included 'Let's Talk About Living' (1960), 'Leader of the Laundromat' (1964) and 'All I Have Left is Johnny's Hubcap' (1962).

Quiz 4

Last Rites

We close the lid on funerary affairs with a round-up
of fatal kisses and near misses. But be warned:
you may have to dig deep.

Answers page 255

1.   Rod Stewart and The Damned's Dave Vanian both had the same job prior to becoming famous. What was it?

2.   As one half of a successful duo, this nutty-sounding singer racked up hit after hit in the Eighties. But in 2005, a motorbike crash left him with all his ribs cracked, a collapsed lung and one broken shoulder, along with major brain injuries. He's still going, non-stop – but who is he?

3.   Ex-Pantera guitarist Dimebag Darrell's life was unexpectedly cut short onstage in December 2004. What happened to him?
     a) A lighting rig fell on him
     b) He was electrocuted when his guitar touched a live wire
     c) He was shot

4.   Bob Geldof had few reasons to be cheerful in 1998, when he erroneously announced the death of one singer live on his XFM radio show. Who was the not-dead-yet artist?

5.   An urban myth developed in the late 1960s that one of The Beatles had died and been replaced by a lookalike. Who?

6.   In May 2006, the wife of one major rock star began receiving condolences from friends over her husband's death. The following year, someone added a death date to his Wikipedia entry. He's a fighter, though, and he's stuck around. But who is he?

7.   As of 2019, who is the highest-earning dead pop star, according to Forbes?
     a) Elvis Presley
     b) Michael Jackson
     c) Bob Marley

8.   Captain Sensible wrote the instrumental opening of The Damned's 'Smash It Up' in tribute to a deceased star whom the band had toured with. Name him.

9.   We kid you not: within three years of their first UK No.1 in 1980, this band had lost its guitarist and bassist to drug overdoses. Name the group.

10. **Which rapper *didn't* die after being robbed and shot at his studio in New York in 1994?**
    a) Tupac Shakur
    b) Snoop Dogg
    c) Ice-T

11. **What was the title of rocker Eddie Cochran's posthumous UK No.1 in 1960?**
    a) 'You'll Miss Me When I'm Gone'
    b) 'Three Steps to Heaven'
    c) 'It's Hard to Say Goodbye'

12. **Bing Crosby, Stevie Ray Vaughan, John Lennon, Marc Bolan and Freddie Mercury all crossed paths with this singer – and all died before him. Name him.**

13. **Latin pop goddess Selena was shot dead by Yolanda Saldívar in 1995. Was the murderer …**
    a) Selena's stylist
    b) Selena's secretary
    c) The head of Selena's fan club

14. **The drummer for which British rock band lost his left arm in a car accident in 1984?**

15. **What was the last Hank Williams song to be released during the country singer's life?**
    a) 'I'll Never Get Out of This World Alive'
    b) 'Never Again (Will I Knock on Your Door)'
    c) 'I Won't Be Home No More'

16. **The '27 Club' is one you wouldn't want to join – only stars who died at that age are welcome. Which of the following *isn't* in the club?**
    a) Jimi Hendrix
    b) Amy Winehouse
    c) Sid Vicious

SAY WHAT?

'I'm going to leave my body to medical science fiction.'
Lemmy (*The Independent*, 14 October 2005)

MOVING PICTURES

Quiz 1

I Hear a New World

Movies and music have gone hand in hand since the days of the silent screen. From bespoke orchestral suites to favourite tracks drawn from a director's record collection, music is an invaluable part of the cinematic experience. So: you think you know the score?

Answers page 256

1. Which Quentin Tarantino movie opened to the strains of 'Misirlou' by Dick Dale and His Del-Tones?

2. Which nostalgic 1973 George Lucas teen movie, set in 1962, spawned a best-selling soundtrack?

3. Which Sixties band's music features prominently in Francis Ford Coppola's *Apocalypse Now* (1979)?

4. Which duo's music was featured on the soundtrack for *The Graduate* (1967)?

5. Which rock musician scored *There Will Be Blood* (2007), *Norwegian Wood* (2010) and *The Master* (2012)?

6. Ralph Stanley's harrowing, unaccompanied rendition of 'O Death' is a stand-out track from which 2000 Coen Brothers movie?

7. What's the best-selling movie soundtrack of all time?
    a) *Saturday Night Fever* (1977)
    b) *Grease* (1978)
    c) *The Bodyguard* (1992)

8. *Requiem for a Dream* (2000) and *Moon* (2009) were both scored by Clint Mansell. Name the band he was in before becoming a film composer.

9. In which movie did Bill Haley and His Comets' 'Rock Around the Clock' first appear?
    a) *Blackboard Jungle* (1955)
    b) *Rock, Rock, Rock!* (1956)
    c) *The Girl Can't Help It* (1957)

10. Who starred in, and sang the title track of, 1972's *The Harder They Come*?

11. Which artist oversaw the soundtrack (as opposed to the score) for 2018's *Black Panther*?

12. Which electronica outfit provided the soundtrack for *Tron: Legacy* (2010)?

13.   Public Enemy sampled Buffalo Springfield's best-known song
      for the title track of which 1998 movie?

14.   Salt-N-Pepa, Eric B. & Rakim and Cypress Hill all appeared on
      the soundtrack for a 1992 crime drama starring Tupac Shakur
      – who, curiously, didn't contribute to the music. Name the film.

15.   For which movie did Seu Jorge contribute cover versions
      of David Bowie songs in Portuguese?

16.   Which movie was accompanied by the first commercially
      released soundtrack?
      a) *Snow White and the Seven Dwarfs*
      b) *The Wizard of Oz*
      c) *High Noon*

DID YOU KNOW?
Sam Smith's 'Writing's on the Wall', from the movie *Spectre* (2015),
was the first theme song from a James Bond movie to hit No.1 in the UK.

Quiz 2

Video Killed the Radio Star

Promo films for new singles had been around since the Sixties, but the pop video as we know it truly came of age in the 1980s. Since then, it's evolved into a multifaceted form, offering the artist unprecedented opportunities for self-expression – not to mention ego pampering.

Answers page 257

1. Which Björk video sees her singing on the back of a flatbed truck driving through Manhattan?

2. In which video does Missy Elliott sport an inflated bin-liner jumpsuit?

3. Aardman Animations contributed to a video that set a record for the most MTV Video Music Awards in 1987 that still stands. Name it.

4. Which Beastie Boys video parodied Seventies cop dramas?

5. In which Kendrick Lamar video is there a recreation of Leonardo da Vinci's *The Last Supper*?

6. Which OutKast video parodies The Beatles' appearance on *The Ed Sullivan Show* in 1964?

7. A hybrid live/pencil-sketch video by Steve Barron won six MTV Video Music Awards in 1986. Name the song and the artist.

8. REM's 'Everybody Hurts' video nods to the start of which classic Sixties movie?
   a) *Blow Out*
   b) *8½*
   c) *La Dolce Vita*

9. Who directed the video for Fatboy Slim's 'Weapon of Choice', featuring a dancing (and occasionally airborne) Christopher Walken?

10. What was unusual about George Michael's video for 'Freedom '90'?
    a) It runs in reverse
    b) He isn't in it
    c) All the parts are played by lookalike celebrities

11. Supermodel Christy Turlington appeared in which Duran Duran video as a teenager?

12. Nirvana's unsettling 'Heart-Shaped Box' video includes a crucifixion and a young girl in KKK-like robes reaching for foetuses on trees. Which photographer directed it?

13. Which Taylor Swift video references Kanye West's interruption of her acceptance speech at the 2009 MTV Video Music Awards?

14. Who directed the video for Red Hot Chili Peppers' 'Under the Bridge'?

   a) Jim Jarmusch
   b) David Lynch
   c) Gus Van Sant

15. How much did it cost to make Michael Jackson's 'Thriller' video?
   a) $500,000
   b) $750,000
   c) $1 million

16. The video for Godley and Creme's song 'Cry' (1985) featured a distinctive effect whereby one person's face cross-fades into someone else's. Among the videos it inspired were 'Black or White' (1991), by Michael Jackson. By what name is this effect best known?

DID YOU KNOW?
The video for Britney Spears's '... Baby One More Time' was filmed at the Venice High School in Los Angeles – the same location where the 1978 movie *Grease* was shot.

Quiz 3

If You Will, Rockumentary

From fly-on-the-wall landmarks such as *Don't Look Back* to the timeless *This Is Spinal Tap*, music docs show our pin-ups at their apex and nadir. They can even offer an unexpected lifeline to bands currently languishing in the 'Where Are They Now?' file (hi, Bros!).

Answers page 258

1. Which kind of musicians were the subject of Morgan Neville's Oscar-winning *20 Feet from Stardom* (2013)?

2. In *This Is Spinal Tap* (1984), what was the name of the band's original incarnation?

3. Which band was the subject of *Starshaped* (1993)?

4. The same siblings who filmed The Beatles' first US jaunt in *What's Happening! The Beatles in the USA* (1964) also captured The Rolling Stones' ill-fated 1969 US tour in *Gimme Shelter* (1970). Name them.

5. Which 2004 documentary traces the contrasting fortunes of The Dandy Warhols and The Brian Jonestown Massacre?

6. Whose first US tour does *D.O.A.: A Rite of Passage* (1980) document?

7. Whose 2004 documentary was subtitled 'Some Kind of Monster'?

8. *Don't Look Back* (1967) starts with a pioneering pop video – for which Bob Dylan song?

9. Grandmaster Flash, Afrika Bambaataa and DJ Shadow all feature in which 2001 hip hop doc?

10. In *Searching for Sugar Man* (2012), what is the titular cult hero's real name?

11. Name any two of the three iconic guitarists whose careers are explored in 2008's *It Might Get Loud*.

12. Grant Gee documented Radiohead's OK Computer Tour with which 1998 movie?

13. Name the director of classic rock docs *Monterey Pop* (1968), *Ziggy Stardust and the Spiders from Mars* (1973) and *101* (1989).

14. Which charismatic but fatally flawed jazz trumpeter was the subject of Bruce Weber's *Let's Get Lost* (1988)?

15. How was the Beastie Boys' doc *Awesome; I Fuckin' Shot That!* (2006) filmed?

16. Which of the following stars didn't perform onstage with The Band in *The Last Waltz* (1978)?
a) Joni Mitchell
b) Ronnie Wood
c) George Harrison

SAY WHAT?

'[Madonna] doesn't want to live off-camera, much less talk. There's nothing to say off-camera. Why would you say something if it's off-camera? What point is there existing?' Warren Beatty, in *Madonna: Truth or Dare* (1991)

Quiz 4

Everyone's Gone to the Movies

Since the dawn of pop, successful singers have straddled parallel movie careers, if only to cash in on their fleeting fame while the going's good. The best of them make the medium their own, however, gaining kudos and even the odd Academy Award in the process. Ready for your screen test?

Answers page 259

1. Which singer more than justified his presence with a supporting role in David Fincher's *The Social Network* (2010)?

2. Name two singers who have taken the female lead role in the various versions of the movie *A Star Is Born*.

3. Which Seventies road movie paired Beach Boy Dennis Wilson with singer-songwriter James Taylor?

4. Which rapper played a police detective in *New Jack City* (1991)?

5. Which of the following didn't feature Mark Wahlberg?
    a) *The Basketball Diaries*
    b) *The Departed*
    c) *Rise of the Planet of the Apes*

6. Which Elvis Presley movie was loosely based on the novel *A Stone for Danny Fisher* by Harold Robbins?

7. Name the 1973 Western starring Kris Kristofferson in a titular role.

8. Pair the singer with the movie:
    a) David Bowie   1) *The Bone Collector*
    b) Queen Latifah   2) *200 Cigarettes*
    c) Elvis Costello   3) *The Last Temptation of Christ*

9. Which singer won an Academy Award for his appearance in *From Here to Eternity* (1953)?
    a) Dean Martin
    b) Frank Sinatra
    c) Merle Travis

10. Ice Cube appeared in which acclaimed Nineties ghetto-based drama?

11. Which cult singer demonstrated his acting chops in *Rumble Fish* (1983), *The Fisher King* (1991) and *Short Cuts* (1993), among other movies?

12. Who was 'out of sight' with George Clooney in the 1998 movie of the same name?

13. Which hip hop star made his movie debut with 1992's *Where the Day Takes You*?

14. Who starred alongside Tupac Shakur in *Poetic Justice* (1993)?

15. Which 2016 movie starred Janelle Monáe as a NASA number-cruncher?

16. *The People vs. Larry Flynt* (1996) and *Man on the Moon* (1999) starred which controversial musician?

SAY WHAT?

'Even in N.W.A. we used to watch stuff like *E.T.* I used to love *Home Alone*, you know what I mean? If I just did hard stuff, that's not keeping it real to me, and I'm all about being real.' Ice Cube (*Time Out*, 6 August 2012)

FORMED A BAND

Quiz 1

The Singer Not the Song

Whether it's rock, pop, rap or reggae, whoever
has the mic calls the tune. Standing out front,
they're the focus of the fans' adulation (and
a magnet for resentment from the rest of the band).
Testing, testing, 1–2–3 …

Answers page 260

1. Manfred Mann's singer Paul Jones had the chance to join another R&B-based band in 1962, but turned it down. Who were they?

2. His real name is Christopher Brian Bridges. But his stage name sounds ridiculous. What is it?

3. Which neighbourly sounding singer turned down 'Toxic', subsequently a major Britney Spears hit?

4. Jimmy Page offered him the chance to become Led Zeppelin's singer, but he turned them down, nominating his friend Robert Plant instead. Name him.

5. With which Eighties pop group did Stephen 'Tin Tin' Duffy once sing?

6. Who was Iron Maiden's original singer?

7. Who did Jeff Buckley refer to as 'my Elvis'?

8. Who has had the most consecutive US No.1 singles?
    a) Whitney Houston
    b) Taylor Swift
    c) Beyoncé

9. In the history of the UK singles chart, only one female singer has ever replaced herself at No.1. Name her.
    a) Rihanna
    b) Taylor Swift
    c) Ariana Grande

10. Which legendary crooner wrote to George Michael in 1990 telling him off for 'wasting his talent'?

11. Flo Rida and T-Pain collaborated on the highest-selling US single of the 2000s. Name it.

12. **Which singer has spent the most cumulative weeks at No.1 on the *Billboard* Hot 100?**
    a) Madonna
    b) Michael Jackson
    c) Elvis Presley

13. **Andre Romelle Young is this rapper's real name. By what pseudonym is he better known?**
    a) André 3000
    b) Dr. Dre
    c) Soulja Boy

14. **What's the name of Dizzee Rascal's Mercury Prize-winning album?**

15. **Who was the most searched-for celebrity in the Noughties?**
    a) Britney Spears
    b) Madonna
    c) Michael Jackson

16. **Which singer has debuted in the US Top 10 most times?**
    a) Rihanna
    b) Lady Gaga
    c) Drake

SAY WHAT?
'I was the blond, fey one who really wanted to be from California, but unfortunately came from West Bromwich.' Robert Plant (*Uncut*, July 2002)

Quiz 2

Careful with That Axe, Eugene

Fretboard wizards have been an integral part of pop
since Robert Johnson allegedly made a deal with the
Horned One at a Mississippi crossroads. From metal
shredders to pop-friendly pickers, we salute
the plank-spankers par excellence.

Answers page 261

1. Who replaced Eric Clapton in The Yardbirds?

2. In his pre-fame days, this guitarist worked as an upholsterer and reportedly inserted some of his own vinyl records into furniture he was refurbishing. Name him.

3. 'Kelly Johnson, on a good day, is as good as Jeff Beck in his rock'n'roll days. She's a fucking brilliant guitar player.' Motörhead's Lemmy there, but which band was the masterly Johnson a member of?

4. Where did Jimi Hendrix first set fire to his guitar?
   a) Finsbury Park Astoria, London
   b) Monterey Pop Festival, California
   c) Cafe Wha?, Greenwich Village, New York

5. What career-threatening accident befell Black Sabbath guitarist Tony Iommi when he was 17?

6. Which Miles Davis sideman went on to lead the Mahavishnu Orchestra?

7. Which guitarist formed Megadeth after leaving Metallica?

8. Which guitarist left Red Hot Chili Peppers in 1992 but rejoined in 1998, staying with the band until 2009?

9. For which 1950s rock'n'roll legend did Cliff Gallup play guitar?
   a) Fats Domino
   b) Gene Vincent
   c) Little Richard

10. Born Ellas Otha Bates, and later known as Ellas McDaniel, he pioneered a distinctive rock'n'roll beat that bears the name by which he became famous. Name that name.

11. He's played with Electronic, The The and The Cribs among many others, but is best known for his first band, who split up in 1987. Name him, and them.

12.   Before he was a Seahorse, this guitarist was a Stone Rose. Name him.

13.   By what cutting-edge name is Saul Hudson better known?

14.   Long before Jimi Hendrix, this blues guitarist played his guitar with his teeth, sometimes behind his back, and sometimes while doing the splits. Who was he?

15.   Who played guitars called 'Cloud' and 'Love Symbol'?

16.   Who was Elvis Presley's original guitar player?

SAY WHAT?

'I'm OK, I'm not technically good, but I can make it fucking howl and move. I was rhythm guitarist. It's an important job. I can make a band drive.' John Lennon (*Rolling Stone*, 21 January 1971)

Quiz 3

The Low End Theory

Four strings is no barrier to virtuosity – step forward
Jaco Pastorius, John Entwistle or Bernard Edwards.
Let's see if you're truly the ace of bass ...

Answers page 262

1. By what name is Michael Peter Balzary better known?

2. Her bass-playing graces some of the Sixties' defining releases, including The Monkees' 'I'm a Believer', Nancy Sinatra's 'These Boots Are Made for Walkin'', The Beach Boys' *Pet Sounds* and *Freak Out!* by the Frank Zappa-fronted Mothers of Invention. Name her.

3. He played with Parliament-Funkadelic, James Brown and his own Rubber Band. Name him.

4. Motown's in-house studio bassist played (uncredited) on a string of hits during the 1960s and early 1970s, and topped *Bass Player Magazine*'s poll of the greatest bassists ever in 2017. Name that bassist.
   a) Chuck Rainey
   b) James Jamerson
   c) Billy Cox

5. Name the shaven-headed bassist who toured with David Bowie from the mid-1990s until his death.

6. AC/DC's bassist retired in 2016, having joined the band in 1977. Who is he?

7. She stepped in when Hole's bassist Kristen Pfaff died, and later toured with Smashing Pumpkins. Name her.

8. Who was The Damned's first bassist?

9. In 1977, Cheap Trick's bassist began playing a new bass, the 'Hamer Quad'. What was so different about it?
   a) It was transparent
   b) It had four necks
   c) It had 12 strings

10. What make of bass did Motörhead's Lemmy play?
    a) Rickenbacker
    b) Fender
    c) Ibanez

11. **Who played the distinctive bassline on Lou Reed's 1972 hit 'Walk on the Wild Side'?**
    a) Mick Ronson
    b) Herbie Flowers
    c) Ian Hunter

12. **Which company produced the first mass-produced solid-bodied electric bass guitar?**
    a) Fender
    b) Gibson
    c) Gretsch

13. **Which William is widely credited with creating the first fretless bass?**
    a) Bill Black
    b) Bill Laswell
    c) Bill Wyman

14. **Who is The Breeders' bass-playing singer?**

15. **Who brought his funky pops and slaps to both Sly and the Family Stone and Graham Central Station?**
    a) Larry Graham
    b) Graham Lewis
    c) Graham Gouldman

16. **He played bass on Kendrick Lamar's *To Pimp a Butterfly* (2015) and released a solo album, *Drunk*, in 2017. His parents named him Stephen Lee Bruner, but he's better know as … what?**

SAY WHAT?

'I don't think of myself as a musician. I'm more of a visual artist who happens to play the bass. I picked up the bass kind of post-punk-style. There's a real art to not learning how to play an instrument and being able to still play it.'
Kim Gordon (*Time Out New York*, 1 July 2008)

Quiz 4

We Got the Beat

Drummers are often the butt of unfair musician jokes, but along with bassists they're the engine room of any group. And they're more than capable of out-rock'n'rolling the rest of the band too (exhibit A: Keith Moon). But are you playing with a full kit? Para-riddle-diddle me this ...

Answers page 263

1. Which rock drummer owned a kit that could take off and rotate in the air above the stage while he continued to play?

2. Clyde Stubblefield played the original drum part in which much-sampled track?
   a) 'Amen, Brother'
   b) 'Apache'
   c) 'Funky Drummer'

3. What then unusual feature did Keith Moon's 'Pictures of Lily' drum kit have?
   a) Two bass drums
   b) Two drum stools
   c) Two gongs

4. Who was the subject of the 2012 documentary *Beware of Mr. Baker*? And what was his most famous group?

5. Who was the drummer with famed Los Angeles studio session musicians The Wrecking Crew?

6. This Afrobeat legend played with Fela Kuti and, more recently, in The Good, the Bad & the Queen with Damon Albarn and Paul Simonon. Name him.

7. Who was Bob Marley's long-serving drummer?
   a) Aston 'Family Man' Barrett
   b) Carlton Barrett
   c) Bunny Wailer

8. Dubbed 'the human metronome', this drummer helped create the 'Motorik' beat that became a defining characteristic of so-called Krautrock. Name him – and, for a bonus point, name his band.

9. With which band did Tony McCarroll drum before being fired in 1995?

10. Who was the drummer on Prince's Sign o' the Times Tour (as seen in the eponymous 1987 concert movie)?

11. Who drums on Stevie Wonder's 'Superstition'?

12. **Who played the drums in prog-rockers Emerson, Lake and Palmer?**
    a) Keith Emerson
    b) Greg Lake
    c) Carl Palmer

13. **For which disco group did Tony Thompson drum?**

14. **Which drummer regularly played a solo dubbed 'Moby Dick' – sometimes lasting up to half an hour – during his band's set? And if you know that, you'll know his band too …**

15. **Which future Rainbow drummer scored a UK Top 3 hit with the instrumental 'Dance with the Devil' in 1974?**

16. **With which influential band did Maureen 'Mo' Tucker drum?**

SAY WHAT?

'Meg White … [is] one of my favourite drummers! She's my daughter's favourite drummer, too. My daughter plays drums to two types of music: White Stripes and AC/DC. I'm like, "That's exactly what you need to be doing."' Dave Grohl (*Rolling Stone*, 29 June 2018)

Quiz 5

Big
Boss Man

'There's no sex and drugs for Ian ... Do you know what I do? I find lost luggage. I locate mandolin strings in the middle of Austin!' Those lines from *Spinal Tap*'s Ian Faith struck a chord with managers everywhere. So how well do you know the men (and women) behind the scenes? Let's talk percentages ...

Answers page 264

1. Dubbed 'the Al Capone of Pop', he once dangled fellow manager Robert Stigwood out of a fourth-storey window when he suspected that he was trying to steal one of his acts. Name the dangler – and, if you can, the act.

2. The daughter of the answer to question no.1 went on to manage a big metal star. Name her – and him.

3. Which of these bands did Malcolm McLaren *not* manage?
   a) Bow Wow Wow
   b) New York Dolls
   c) X-Ray Spex

4. He worked as a bouncer at Soho's famous 2i's Coffee Bar, as a wrestler under the monikers 'Count Massimo' and 'Count Bruno Alassio of Milan' and served time as an extra and stuntman on TV and in movies, including *The Guns of Navarone* (1961). Then, in the late 1960s, he started managing one of the biggest rock bands of all time. Name him.

5. Which rock star did Tony Defries manage from 1970 to 1975?

6. Kit Lambert and Chris Stamp managed The Who from their early days into the 1970s. One of them had a brother who was a famous actor – name that thespian sibling.

7. Who managed Bob Dylan until 1970?

8. Which boy band did Lou Pearlman manage?
   a) Backstreet Boys
   b) Boyz II Men
   c) New Kids on the Block

9. Which band did Allen Klein *not* manage?
   a) The Beatles
   b) The Rolling Stones
   c) Bee Gees

10. Who severed ties with manager Mathew Knowles in 2011? And for an extra point, why might that have been rather awkward?

11. In a concert review in 1974, a *Rolling Stone* writer enthused, 'I saw rock and roll future and its name is Bruce Springsteen.' Putting his money where his pen was, he went on to manage 'The Boss'. What is his name?

12. Amy Winehouse, Annie Lennox and the Spice Girls were all managed by the same man – who also created the TV talent franchise *American Idol*. Name him.

13. He manages PJ Harvey and The Rapture now, but which rock band did Paul McGuinness handle from 1978 to 2013?

14. Justin Bieber, Ariana Grande and Carly Rae Jepsen all share the same manager. Who is he?
    a) Zach Quillen
    b) Troy Carter
    c) Scooter Braun

15. For more than 30 years, René Angélil was the husband and manager of one of history's most successful singers. Think twice, then name her.

16. George du Maurier's novel *Trilby* (1895) features a character who seduces and manipulates a gifted young singer, turning her into a famous star. His name has become a byword for exploitative managers ever since – what is it?

SAY WHAT?

'Writing a song like "Anarchy in the U.K." is definitely a statement of intent … It's a call to arms to the kids who believe very strongly that rock and roll was taken away from them. And now it's coming back.' Malcolm McLaren, then manager of the Sex Pistols (*NME*, 27 November 1976)

Quiz 6

We Are Family

Tangled lines of lineage have run through popular music forever. Band members quit, join other bands, rejoin their first group, growing a trail of family trees as they do. But how well do you know your pop ancestry?

Answers page 265

1. Which musician links the following bands: The Cure, Siouxsie and the Banshees, The Glove.

2. An early line-up of Bow Wow Wow included a certain 'Lieutenant Lush', who went on to cultured success a few years later under another pseudonym. Name him.

3. Liverpool's short-lived band The Crucial Three included the front men of three bands who went on to enjoy chart success in the 1980s. Name one of them.

4. Eric Clapton, Mick Taylor, Jack Bruce, Peter Green, Mick Fleetwood and John McVie all played with a particular British blues band before going on to join more successful groups. Name that band.

5. Bad Company originally featured Paul Rodgers (vocals), Simon Kirke (drums), Mick Ralphs (guitar) and Boz Burrell (bass), all ex-members of three big rock acts of the early 1970s. Name any one of those parent bands.

6. Electric Light Orchestra arose out of the ashes of a famous Sixties band, and initially featured three members from it. Name the band – and, if you can, the three musicians.

7. Who replaced Murray Dalglish as drummer with The Jesus and Mary Chain?

8. He'd done stints in The Bluebells, Aztec Camera and The Colourfield, but is best remembered for a brief stint in 1986 as second guitarist with an iconic British band. Who is he?

9. Jane's Addiction have at various points included an ex-Red Hot Chili Pepper and an ex-member of Guns N' Roses. Name either of them.

10. When Small Faces' vocalist unexpectedly quit in 1968, they recruited two members of The Jeff Beck Group instead. One would go on to stellar success as a solo artist, the other would join the 'greatest rock'n'roll band in the world'. Name them.

11. Tina Weymouth and Chris Frantz set up their own band while still members of Talking Heads. Name it.

12. The Other Two are a splinter group from which better-known band?

13. Name any of the acts Norman Cook was associated with between his time as bassist in The Housemartins and his reinvention as big-beat guru Fatboy Slim.

14. Who has fronted The Boys Next Door, The Birthday Party and Grinderman?

15. Which musician links Ride, Oasis and Beady Eye?

16. Which band did Terry Hall, Neville Staple and Lynval Golding form after leaving The Specials in 1981?

DID YOU KNOW?
Around 66 musicians played in The Fall, from the band's inception in 1976 to the death of singer (and sole continuous member) Mark E. Smith in 2018.

FESTIVALS

Quiz 1

Were You There?

There's nothing quite like living in a pop-up town for a long weekend, where you can buy overpriced, undercooked food, sleep in mud and possibly see the best gig of your life. On which subject ...

Answers page 266

1. On the Saturday afternoon at 1967's Monterey International Pop Festival, one act played such a scorching set that they were invited back to repeat the performance so that it could be captured for the documentary of the event. They were the only act to play twice that weekend. Name that act.
   a) Big Brother and the Holding Company (featuring Janis Joplin)
   b) The Who
   c) The Jimi Hendrix Experience

2. Which singer made a triumphant appearance at Monterey International Pop Festival in 1967 – where he dubbed the audience 'the love crowd' – but died unexpectedly six months later?

3. What made Bob Marley's appearance at the Smile Jamaica Concert – a free festival on 5 December 1976 – particularly remarkable?

4. At which 1969 festival did Bob Dylan make his first major public appearance since his motorcycle crash in 1966?

5. In 1970, another Sixties legend played his last UK gig at the same festival, dying just three weeks after appearing onstage there. Name him.

6. Who appeared naked onstage at the 1993 Lollapalooza, save for black tape over their mouths and a black circle over their genitals, in a protest against censorship in music?
   a) Red Hot Chili Peppers
   b) Jane's Addiction
   c) Rage Against the Machine

7. At Coachella in 2008, one artist creamed all the other acts with covers of The B-52s' 'Rock Lobster', The Beatles' 'Come Together' and Radiohead's 'Creep'. The crowd were delirious. Who was it?

8. Which star joined band Semi Precious Weapons on drums in 2010 at Lollapalooza, then snogged the lead singer before stage diving – and all while sporting a fishnet body stocking and pasties?

9.   In 2009, The Cure's set at Coachella ended abruptly: their sound was cut during 'Boys Don't Cry' when they ran over the allotted curfew time. What happened next?
a) They trashed their instruments onstage
b) A fan helped get the sound up and running again
c) The crowd finished off the set by singing the rest of the song

10. 'I think maybe that was my favourite Glastonbury moment of all time', said the festival's founder Michael Eavis in 2016. What was he referring to?
a) The Rolling Stones playing 'Sympathy for the Devil' in 2013
b) David Bowie finishing his 2000 set with an encore of '"Heroes"'
c) A reunited Blur playing an emotional 'Tender' in 2009

11. At one 2012 festival, Snoop Dogg and Dr. Dre were joined onstage by a hologram of Tupac Shakur, who had died just over 15 years earlier. Name the festival.

12. At Glastonbury in 2014, which performer regaled the crowd by playing the theme from *The Benny Hill Show* – twice – on a rhinestone-encrusted saxophone?

13. At which festival did Nine Inch Nails take to the stage covered in mud?

14. At one point during The Stooges' set at 1970's Cincinnati Pop Festival, Iggy Pop stood on the outstretched hands of the fans and smeared himself with ... what?
a) Blood
b) Whipped cream
c) Peanut butter

15. What unconventional sound-system transport did Super Furry Animals take with them on a festival tour in 1996?

16. How did Prodigy's Keith Flint make his stage entrance at Glastonbury in 1995?
a) In a giant glass 'hamster' ball
b) On a horse
c) Lowered down on a trapeze

Quiz 2

Three Days of Peace & Music

Woodstock seemed to bookend that optimistic decade so neatly, hosting some of the decade's most inspirational acts and catching the Sixties dream while it was still alive. Remarkably, despite endless traffic jams to the site, food shortages, a heavy thunderstorm and reports of bad brown acid, there was no violence. The vibrations stayed good.

Answers page 267

1. Woodstock was the biggest festival in history. True or false?

2. The first band to sign up for the festival ended up having to play in the early hours of Sunday morning. Maybe they were born under a bad moon ... Who were they?
a) Creedence Clearwater Revival
b) Jefferson Airplane
c) The Incredible String Band

3. When the opening acts became bogged down in heavy traffic, which singer-songwriter opened the festival with a solo set – including a completely improvised song, 'Freedom', that later became a hit?
a) Arlo Guthrie
b) Richie Havens
c) Tim Hardin

4. And who closed the festival, on the morning of Monday, 18 August 1969?

5. At the end of The Who's set, in the early hours of Sunday, 17 August, what did Pete Townshend do with his guitar?
a) He smashed it
b) He set light to it
c) He threw it into the audience

6. In the Academy Award-winning documentary *Woodstock* (1970), 20-year-old Michael Shrieve is shown playing a jaw-dropping drum solo. With which band was he playing? And for an extra point, in which song does his solo feature?

7. Which rock'n'roll revival group appeared as the penultimate act of the festival?

8. Which singer did the Kozmic Blues Band back, on Sunday, 17 August?

9. John B. Sebastian played a five-song solo set at Woodstock, having left the band that made him famous the previous year. Name that band.

10. Who played the anti-Vietnam song 'I-Feel-Like-I'm-Fixin'-to-Die Rag' – still his best-known tune – at Woodstock?

11. **Which of the following acts didn't play at Woodstock?**
    a) Sly and the Family Stone
    b) Santana
    c) The Doors

12. **Internationally renowned sitarist Ravi Shankar said he found the whole experience 'terrifying'. What did he say the crowd reminded him of?**
    a) Lost piglets roaming around a sty
    b) Water buffaloes in India
    c) Hippos in mud baths

13. **What was the last song to be heard at Woodstock?**

14. **The hit song 'Woodstock' was penned by a songwriter whose manager had advised her not to go to the festival. Her boyfriend filled her in on it afterwards and she based the song on his impressions. Name her. And for an extra point, name him.**

15. **Which young film-maker served as assistant director on the 1970 documentary *Woodstock*?**
    a) Francis Ford Coppola
    b) Martin Scorsese
    c) Peter Bogdanovich

16. **Owing to the overwhelming number of attendees, the organizers were forced to make the event, which was originally ticketed, a free festival. They nearly went bankrupt. It took more than a decade for them to make their money back. How in debt were they?**
    a) Around $400,000
    b) Around $800,000
    c) Around $1.4 million

SAY WHAT?

Melvyn Bragg (interviewer): 'Woodstock ... was one of the biggest pop events in world terms ... What did it change?'
Pete Townshend: 'Well, it changed me. I hated it.' (*South Bank Show*, 1974)

Quiz 3

Going Up the Country

It drew an attendance of around 1,500 at its first outing, but these days Glastonbury Festival creates the second-largest population in Somerset whenever it's staged. From its folksy roots, it now welcomes world-famous hip hop and R&B stars alongside superstar DJs and rock royalty.

Answers page 268

1. What was the ticket price for the original Glastonbury Festival in 1970?

2. Who headlined that inaugural event?

3. In 1995, The Stone Roses were forced to pull out of their headlining slot because guitarist John Squire broke a collarbone while cycling. Who replaced them?

4. Which boy-band star joined Oasis onstage during their set that year?

5. Who headlined Glastonbury's Pyramid Stage on the Friday night in 2007?

6. At Glastonbury Festival in 2015, a prankster invaded the stage during a performance by which musician?

7. How much do residents of Pilton, a village near the Glastonbury farm, pay for admittance to the festival?
    a) Nothing – it's free to them
    b) £1
    c) £5

8. When did a permanent Pyramid Stage become a fixture at Glastonbury?
    a) 1971
    b) 1981
    c) 1991

9. The Classical Tent made its debut at the festival in 1986. Name the well-known film composer who curated the show there.

10. Suzanne Vega and her bassist had received death threats prior to their appearance at the festival in 1989. What protective steps did she take?
    a) She played behind a screen of bullet-proof glass
    b) She wore a bullet-proof vest
    c) She changed the time and date of her set at the last minute

11. In 1999, Manic Street Preachers brought their own toilets, complete with a notice stipulating that they were for their own private use. It prompted the comment 'That's a nice socialist gesture, lads' – from which singer-songwriter?

12. News of Michael Jackson's death hit festival-goers at the 2009 event. Various tributes were paid. What did Lily Allen wear to mark MJ's passing?

13. In 2010, which Doctor Who actor joined Orbital onstage for their remix of the show's theme tune?

14. Who became the first solo female artist in more than 20 years to headline at Glastonbury in 2011?

15. When Dave Grohl broke his leg a few weeks before Foo Fighters were due to headline the festival on the Friday night in 2015, which act stepped in to fill their shoes?

16. Also in 2015, Patti Smith interrupted her set to wheel on a birthday cake for an illustrious 80-year-old spiritual figure who was visiting the festival that year. Name him.

SAY WHAT?

'Someone ought to build a bypass over this shithole.'
Nicky Wire, onstage at Glastonbury, 1994

Quiz 4

Closing Acts

You lost your tent, your friends and your money.
But hang on to your wristband: before you
head home (with your new friends and
a rucksack full of muddy laundry), look what's
just appeared on the main stage!

Answers page 269

1. At Reading Festival in 2004, one rapper appeared onstage 20 minutes late and only lasted a further 20 minutes before being bottled off. Was it ...
    a) Jay-Z
    b) Eminem
    c) 50 Cent

2. Which US alternative music star came up with the concept of touring festival Lollapalooza, which debuted in 1991?
    a) Perry Farrell of Jane's Addiction
    b) Trent Reznor of Nine Inch Nails
    c) Mark Arm of Mudhoney

3. What yellow comic strip character was named after a famous rock festival. And what was the name of the comic strip and its author?

4. What was the USP of Lilith Fair?

5. Which 2016 festival – dubbed 'Oldchella' – had a line-up of The Rolling Stones, Paul McCartney, Bob Dylan, Neil Young, Roger Waters and The Who?

6. There is now an annual underwater festival. True or false?

7. Where is South by Southwest staged?

8. At which festival do painted sheep roam the site?

9. Which festival includes an observatory, from which you can view Jupiter's moons and Saturn's rings?

10. How long did it take EDM festival Tomorrowland to sell out in 2013?
    a) 1 second
    b) 30 seconds
    c) 1 minute

11. For a number of years, Festival No.6 was held in Portmeirion, north Wales. Which cult TV series was filmed there in the 1960s?

12. Coachella first sold out in 2004. Which act headlined that year?

13. This controversial promoter ran the famous Fillmore West and Fillmore East concert venues and in 1973 kick-started the Day on the Green rock festival, which ran until the 1990s. Name him.

14. Which metal festival was held at Castle Donington, UK, from 1980 to 1996?

15. Which musician founded world-music festival WOMAD in 1980?

16. In 1994, a group of pen-pals who met through *NME* inaugurated the Whitby Goth Weekend, which is still running today. Why Whitby?

SAY WHAT?
'We were doing an interview and someone said, "You know you're not supposed to swear – there's no swearing on Glastonbury," he said. I was like, "What the fuck is that supposed to fucking mean?"'
Dave Grohl of Foo Fighters (onstage at Glastonbury Festival, 25 June 2017)

THANK YOU AND GOODNIGHT

Quiz 1

On This Day in History

Think you know your music calendar?
Let's see if you've got a memory for a hot date ...

Answers page 270

1. On 21 May 1971, a legendary soul singer released a ground-breaking LP that took in everything from Vietnam to the stress of contemporary urban living and ecology. His label boss thought it would bomb; it became a huge best-seller. Name the artist and the album.

2. Which concert took place on 13 July 1985?

3. This controversial single, released on 9 August 1988, is generally regarded as announcing the dawn of gangsta rap. Name it.

4. On 24 March 1958, a pivotal event took place in Elvis Presley's life. What was it?
   a) His mother died
   b) He was drafted into the US Army
   c) He officially became the richest singer of all time

5. On 14 August 1995, the UK's two biggest bands released their new singles on the same day. Name them, and the respective songs.

6. Prince's public image took a memorable turn on 7 June 1993. What happened?

7. Freddie Mercury passed away on 24 November 1991. The drummer of a made-up rock band died the same day – name him.

8. Which rock group filed a lawsuit against Napster on 14 April 2000?

9. On 31 July 2018, who became the first black woman to appear on the cover of British *Vogue*?
   a) Rihanna
   b) Beyoncé
   c) Azealia Banks

10. In the *Billboard* Hot 100 dated 14 July 2018, Drake broke a chart record that had stood since 1964. What was it?

11. The Coldplay single released on 13 June 2008 would give them their first US No.1. Name it.

12. What reality TV talent show hit UK screens on 6 October 2001?

13. On 11 December 1961, The Marvelettes' 'Please Mr. Postman' gave a legendary US record label its first US pop No.1. Name that label.

14. ABBA won the Eurovision Song Contest on 6 April 1974 – with which song?

15. The Beatles played their last gig ever on 30 January 1969. Where?

16. What was the name of the benefit concert held on 20 October 2001 in Madison Square Garden, prompted by the 9/11 terrorist attacks?

DID YOU KNOW?
On 13 July 1939, Frank Sinatra made his recording debut.

Quiz 2

The First Cut Is the Deepest

You (literally) can't beat a first. From million sellers to million tweets, we present 16 questions on pioneering pop facts and stats.

Answers page 271

1. Which male and female pop stars were first to have over 100 million Twitter followers?

2. Who won the first Grammy for rap?

3. What makes 'Vesti la giubba' (1902), sung by Enrico Caruso, a significant first?

4. What sales record did *Millennium* (1999), by Backstreet Boys, set?

5. Which act was the first pop group to appear on Channel 5?
   a) Take That
   b) Five Star
   c) Spice Girls

6. Who was the first woman to win a Grammy for Album of the Year twice for her solo albums?

7. What was the first music video aired on MTV?

8. What is generally regarded as the first rock stadium gig?

9. What was the first pop album to be released on CD?

10. What was the first original album to spawn five *Billboard* No.1 singles?

11. Who was the first artist to debut in the *Billboard* Top 10 with two songs in the same week?

12. At the 2019 Grammy Awards, Childish Gambino's 'This Is America' achieved two 'firsts' for a hip hop song. Name either one of them.

13. What was the first foreign-language UK No.1 single?

14.   Westlife's 'I Have a Dream'/'Seasons in the Sun' reached No.1 in the UK in December 1999 and stayed there into the New Year. But what was the first *new* UK No.1 of the 21st century?

15.   Who is the first woman to have a single and album at the top of the US and UK charts simultaneously?
       a) Taylor Swift
       b) Madonna
       c) Beyoncé

16.   What was the first rap album to reach No.1 on the *Billboard* 200 chart?

Quiz 3

Some Might Say

The best pop stars have a happy knack of being eminently quotable. From pop philosophy to frank revelation, vitriol to vanity, let's get this straight ...

Answers page 272

1. 'I've lied so much about the past, I can't even tell myself what is true any more.' Which native New Yorker made that confession?

2. Who told one interviewer in the 1980s, 'The great strength of heavy metal is that it doesn't progress'?

3. Who did St. Vincent refer to as 'a cartoon yeast infection'?
   a) Harvey Weinstein
   b) Donald Trump
   c) R. Kelly

4. Which pop queen once admitted, 'I enjoy being a bitch. I enjoy being surrounded by bitches. I certainly don't go looking for the most perfect people. I'd find that boring'?

5. Who claimed, in 2012, 'I am flawed as a human being ... I am flawed as a person, as a man, I am flawed. But my music is perfect!'

6. In 2010, who claimed 'the internet is over', adding that it's 'like MTV. At one time MTV was hip, and suddenly it became outdated. Anyway, all these computer and digital gadgets are no good. They just fill your head with numbers, and that can't be good for you'?

7. Which singer stated, in 1985, 'I won't be happy till I'm as famous as God.'

8. 'She's gonna look back on some of these moments and go, "Why did I say that?" ... I think that's great. That's what life is. Go out there and make some bad choices, make some mistakes. It's much more exciting than if she was this controlled robot.' Jay-Z is the speaker, but who is he talking about?
   a) Katy Perry
   b) Rihanna
   c) Azealia Banks

9. 'The guitarist I've got a lot of time for. The drummer I've never met – I hear he's a nice guy. The bass player and the singer – I hope the pair of them catch AIDS and die because I fucking hate them two.' Name the speaker – and, for an extra point, the band being dissed.

10.   Which gruff-voiced singer said – on the subject of taking care of his own voice – 'Protect it? From what? Vandals?'

11.   '*You've* seen him go from bad to worse. *I've* seen him go from good to bad to worse.' Who's the speaker – and who are they talking about?
    a) Carl Barat on Pete Doherty
    b) Dave Grohl on Kurt Cobain
    c) John Lydon on Sid Vicious

12.   'I always wanted to be Romeo, not Juliet ... Romeo is a much cooler way to be – Juliet's just up in a balcony, waiting.' Who's the gender-fluid Romeo?
    a) Hélöise Letissier (Christine of Christine and the Queens)
    b) Miley Cyrus
    c) Janelle Monáe

13.   'I don't want people to see I'm a human being. I don't even drink water onstage in front of anybody, because I want them to focus on the fantasy of the music and be transported from where they are to somewhere else. People can't do that if you're just on Earth. We need to go to heaven.' Who's the star speaker?
    a) Lady Gaga
    b) David Bowie
    c) Madonna

14.   'There was a time when I had to take down all the mirrors. I felt I was looking at myself too much. The world made such a big deal of how I looked ... it was problematic.' Name the reflective singer.
    a) Taylor Swift
    b) John Taylor of Duran Duran
    c) Debbie Harry

15.   'I just find it frustrating that people think that I'm some kind of weirdo reclusive that never comes out into the world.' This woman's work makes the waits worthwhile – name her.

Quiz 4

I Know Where Syd Barrett Lives

For every Madonna there's a thousand Judee Sills writing stunning songs but never attaining star status. Some get too many bad breaks, some do too many bad drugs and others simply aren't equipped to deal with the Faustian demands of fame and fortune. So, come join our cult (heroes).

Answers page 273

1. This hip hop producer dropped his acclaimed sophomore studio album *Donuts* three days before his untimely death in 2006. Who was he?

2. Which musician and artist scored a UK No.1 in 1981 with 'O Superman'?

3. The discography of another multimedia artist includes albums *Fly* (1971) and *Season of Glass* (1981), the cover of the latter featuring her dead husband's glasses. Name her.

4. He was a Sixties heartthrob. Then he embarked on an acclaimed solo career making 'challenging' music (on one track he recorded the sound of a lump of meat being punched). He's certainly never made it easy on himself – but who is he?

5. With which pioneering sound design outfit is Delia Derbyshire associated?

6. Which experimental jazz icon led a band he dubbed The Arkestra? And for a bonus point, where did he claim to be from?

7. This revered singer-songwriter found fame with post-rock pioneers Talk Talk. He passed away in 2019, more than 20 years after his sole solo album. Name him.

8. He managed Echo and the Bunnymen and The Teardrop Explodes, was a Timelord and one half of the KLF. Name him.

9. Which 1997 film featured the songwriting talents of Elliott Smith?

10. Unrecognized in his lifetime, this singer-songwriter has since been acknowledged as an influence by The Cure's Robert Smith and REM's Peter Buck, among others. He recorded only three albums before dying of an overdose in 1974. Name him.

11. Which Syd Barrett song gave Pink Floyd their first UK Top 10 hit?

12. This transgressive gender bender advised us to 'Fuck the Pain Away' in 2000 and appeared on the cover of a 2003 album wearing a beard. Name her.

13. Which maverick songwriter wrote timeless melodies for The La's?

14. Since the early 1990s, he's worked under the pseudonyms GAK, The Dice Man, AFX and Polygon Window among others. Along the way, he's produced tracks with snappy titles such as 'fz pseudotimestretch+e+3 [138.85]'. He cares because you do. Name him.

15. He sang The Box Tops' 1967 worldwide No.1 'The Letter', but is better remembered for the albums he made in the early 1970s with another group. He was never a big star, but his band was. Name him.

16. Emerging in the 1980s with a trio of twins, this treasured singer eschewed recognizable language and lyrics, although she was a true phraser. Who is she?

SAY WHAT?

'It is a tragedy – a great tragedy because he was an innovator. One of the three or four greats along with Dylan.' Pink Floyd's David Gilmour, on Syd Barrett (*NME*, 13 April 1974)

Quiz 5

This Is My Truth Tell Me Yours

Given the excess that goes hand in hand with rock'n'roll, it's little wonder urban legends and musical myths spring up. Then again, sometimes the weirdest stories check out after all. Can you sort the gospel from the grime? Are the following statements true or false?

Answers page 274

1. Mama Cass, of The Mamas and the Papas, died from choking on a ham sandwich.

2. The ink used in the first ever Kiss comic book, published in 1977, is infused with the blood of the band members.

3. Dave Gahan once had a coffin-shaped bed.

4. Infamous cult leader Charles Manson once wrote a song recorded by The Beach Boys.

5. The Beatles smoked a joint at Buckingham Palace before receiving their MBE from the Queen in 1965.

6. Keith Moon drove a Rolls-Royce into a swimming pool during his 21st-birthday celebrations.

7. There is a US hotline dedicated to playing Hall & Oates songs.

8. Keith Richards once had a complete blood transfusion in a Swiss clinic.

9. The band 10cc got their name from the average amount of semen emitted in an ejaculation.

10. In 1977, Aerosmith enquired about renting a plane that crashed later that same year, killing several members of Lynyrd Skynyrd.

11. Stevie Nicks damaged her nose so badly from taking cocaine that she had to inject it anally, with the help of a roadie and a straw.

12. Debbie Harry had a narrow escape when she got into a car with serial killer Ted Bundy.

13. Guns N' Roses singer Axl Rose recorded himself having sex with drummer Steven Adler's sometime girlfriend in the studio and used the recording on a GNR track.

14. Jack and Meg White of The White Stripes were brother and sister.

15. Rock group Van Halen stipulated in their contract that as part of their backstage rider they should have a bowl of M&Ms with all the brown ones removed.

16. Joni Mitchell once wore a blackface disguise for an album cover.

SAY WHAT?

'If people don't want to believe that Meg is my sister, that's fine ... If I told you that Meg is my cousin and that she has always been my cousin and I could prove it, people would say that's a lie, too. People won't believe the truth.' Jack White (*Spin*, 2002. *See question 14*)

Quiz 6

Living with the NME

The quizzes have (almost) left the building. But before the lights go up, let's take a final stroll through *NME*'s storied past, as we revisit 16 milestone moments in the celebrated paper's history. And don't forget to buy a T-shirt on the way out.

Answers page 275

1. In July 1976, *NME* journalist Charles Shaar Murray penned an advert seeking 'hip young gunslingers' to write for the paper. Which two journalistic *enfants terribles* joined as a result?

2. An acclaimed selection of one *NME* journalist's work was collected under the title *The Dark Stuff*. Name that writer.

3. In 1989, what score did reviewer David Quantick give to the album *This Is Spinal Tap*, from the movie of the same name?

4. One mouth-watering NME Poll Winners Concert saw appearances by The Beatles, The Rolling Stones, The Animals, The Moody Blues, The Kinks, The Walker Brothers, Them, Tom Jones and Dusty Springfield, among others. In what year?
   a) 1962
   b) 1965
   c) 1968

5. Two revered musical icons tie for the most NME Award wins ever, with 26 each. Name either of them.

6. At its peak, what was the highest average circulation of the print *NME*?
   a) 307,000 plus
   b) 407,000 plus
   c) 507,000 plus

7. The first UK singles chart appeared in the *NME* dated 14 November 1952. What form did the listings take?
   a) Top 10
   b) Top 12
   c) Top 15

8. 'This is quite good. Just,' opined *NME*'s Jack Barron in a 7/10 album review in 1989. By 2006, the same album topped the paper's list of '100 Greatest British Albums Ever'. Name it.

9. Which two artists are tied for the most *NME* covers in a year, with seven each?
   a) T. Rex and Oasis
   b) The Beatles and Morrissey
   c) David Bowie and The Clash

10. One *NME* live review from October 1976 warned, 'This is what your fathers fought to save you from', and griped that the band's 'melodies flowed as slowly as a piece of garbage floating down the polluted Rhine'. The writer was Barry Miles. Who was the act?

11. In the context of *NME*, what links *Random Access Memories* (2013) by Daft Punk, *Let England Shake* (2011) by PJ Harvey, *OK Computer* (1996) by Radiohead and *Generation Terrorists* (1992) by Manic Street Preachers?

12. 'A pop craftsman in the classic tradition and a master of his trade. Of his generation, probably only Kurt Cobain wielded the manipulative power of melody better' (*NME*, 27 August 1994). Name the singer and the album referred to.

13. Stefflon Don was the cover star of the March 2018 *NME*. What made it a landmark issue?

14. In a notorious incident in 1991, Manic Street Preacher Richey Edwards carved '4 Real' into his arm, in front of an *NME* journalist who had been talking with him. Name that hack.

15. The cover of the 8 October 1988 *NME* proclaimed one group as 'the greatest rock'n'roll band in the world?!'. Who was the act in question?

16. In 2014, *NME* writers past and present voted for the all-time greatest pop song. What was the winner?
    a) 'There Is a Light That Never Goes Out', by The Smiths
    b) 'Waterloo Sunset', by The Kinks
    c) 'Smells Like Teen Spirit', by Nirvana

SAY WHAT?

'It's what the music means to you ... not some guy from a magazine waffling on and putting his own fairy tales on it.' Van Morrison (*Uncut*, 2005)

Answers

BEST-SELLERS
Quiz 1: The Number One Song in Heaven

1.   'Crazy', by Gnarls Barkley, on 8 April 2006
2.   c) 'Rock Around the Clock', by Bill Haley and His Comets
3.   'Every Breath You Take' (1983)
4.   True
5.   'Impossible', by James Arthur. Released in 2012, it reached No.1 in the UK and had sold 1.53 million copies as of December 2017
6.   True
7.   'Music', in 2000
8.   Katy Perry. The quintet of chart-toppers came from 2010's *Teenage Dream*
9.   a) Usher, with 41 weeks at No.1
10. 'Another Brick in the Wall (Part 2)', by Pink Floyd
11. Cliff Richard
12. b) 'Happy', by Pharrell Williams, a No.1 in 2013–14
13. a) 'Evergreen', by Will Young. It sold more than 1.1 million copies in 2002
14. 'Vienna', by Ultravox
15. 'The Way I Are', by Timbaland feat. Keri Hilson
16. Either 'One Sweet Day', by Mariah Carey and Boyz II Men (1995), or 'Despacito', by Luis Fonsi and Daddy Yankee feat. Justin Bieber (2017). Both were No.1 for 16 weeks

BEST-SELLERS
Quiz 2: One in Every Home

1. c) *London Calling*
2. Elton John, *The Lion King*
3. *Back in Black* (1980), by AC/DC
4. a) *West Side Story*
5. One Direction
6. *The Sound of Music*
7. Spice Girls
8. b) 25 (2015), by Adele, with first-week sales of 803,000
9. a) 4
10. Coldplay: *Viva la Vida or Death and All His Friends* (2008); U2: *No Line on the Horizon* (2009)
11. False: it was *Out of Time* (1991)
12. *Jagged Little Pill*, by Alanis Morissette
13. *No Strings Attached*, by NSYNC
14. *x* (2014); ÷ (2017)
15. *The Fame* (2008)
16. Simon and Garfunkel. The album was *Bridge Over Troubled Water* (1970)

BEST-SELLERS
Quiz 3: The Winner Takes It All

1. Primal Scream
2. Jarvis Cocker
3. b) 2010
4. Radiohead
5. Jay-Z (Kanye West currently has 21)
6. c) *Slumdog Millionaire* (2008)
7. Elvis Presley
8. The KLF
9. a) Henry Mancini, for *The Music from Peter Gunn*
10. Adele
11. b) *Pinocchio* (1940)
12. *Timeless*, by Goldie (1995)
13. b) Peter Gabriel, with ten in 1987
14. 'Raindrops Keep Fallin' on My Head'
15. a) Metallica, with six wins, including the first three between 1990 and 1992
16. Robbie Williams: 13 as a solo star and a further five with Take That

BEST-SELLERS
Quiz 4: Santa Claus Is Comin' to Town

1. Eartha Kitt
2. a) US president John F. Kennedy was shot. It was 22 November 1963
3. a) *Holiday Inn* (1942)
4. David Bowie. The song was 'Peace on Earth/Little Drummer Boy'
5. 'The Christmas Song (Merry Christmas to You)'
6. c) It was the third of their first three singles to reach No.1 in the UK
7. 'Santa Claus Is Comin' to Town'
8. b) Greg Lake
9. c) 'Fairytale of New York', by The Pogues feat. Kirsty MacColl
10. b) Four: 1984, 1989, 2004 and 2014 (the last two were re-recordings)
11. 'Merry Christmas Everybody', by Slade
12. 'Happy Xmas', by John Lennon, Yoko Ono and Plastic Ono Band with the Harlem Community Choir
13. b) Boney M
14. Jona Lewie
15. Spice Girls, with '2 Become 1' (1996), 'Too Much' (1997) and 'Goodbye' (1998). The Beatles did it three decades beforehand, with 'I Want to Hold Your Hand' (1963), 'I Feel Fine' (1964) and 'We Can Work It Out'/'Day Tripper' (1965)
16. False – despite singer Les Gray's knowingly Elvis-like delivery

BEST-SELLERS
Quiz 5: Cover Me

1. The Byrds
2. 'Step On'. It was a cover of the song originally titled 'He's Gonna Step on You Again', by John Kongos
3. '(I Can't Get No) Satisfaction' (1965)
4. 'Money (That's What I Want)' (1959)
5. 'Knock on Wood'
6. A huge list! The best-known versions are probably by one of the following: John Cale, Jeff Buckley, Alexandra Burke, KD Lang, Rufus Wainwright, Willie Nelson, Susan Boyle, Bono, Regina Spektor, Katherine Jenkins or Kate Voegele
7. 'I Will Always Love You'. Whitney's 1992 version was a 14-week No.1 on *Billboard*
8. The Fall
9. b) Elvis Costello
10. Sex Pistols
11. c) Roberta Flack
12. 'Proud Mary'
13. b) 'Hurt'
14. c) *The Spaghetti Incident?*
15. 'La Vie en Rose'
16. Gloria Jones

BEST-SELLERS
Quiz 6: Once in a Lifetime

1. c) Wild Cherry, in 1976
2. Phil Spector
3. c) Stacy's
4. c) 'Ring My Bell'
5. 'Mickey'
6. 'Don't Worry, Be Happy'
7. b) 'Mambo No.5'
8. Men
9. c) House of Pain
10. 'In the Garden of Eden'
11. Prince
12. 'Rapper's Delight'
13. 'Under Pressure'
14. c) 'Who Let the Dogs Out?'
15. c) *Top of the Pops*
16. 'F.U.R.B. (Fuck You Right Back)', by Frankee

DECADE BY DECADE
Quiz 1: The Fifties

1. Johnnie Ray
2. Hank Williams
3. Jerry Lee Lewis
4. Elvis Presley's 'Jailhouse Rock', in 1957
5. a) W.C. Handy
6. c) Four o'clock
7. c) White
8. Take your pick from the following: 'Hound Dog'/'Don't Be Cruel', by Elvis Presley; 'Love Letters in the Sand', by Pat Boone; 'Rock Around the Clock', by Bill Haley and His Comets; 'The Chipmunk Song', by The Chipmunks; and 'Tom Dooley', by The Kingston Trio
9. a) Danny and The Juniors
10. Eddie Cochran
11. c) Frank Sinatra
12. Choose from: Guy Mitchell, Marty Robbins or Tommy Steele
13. Cliff Richard
14. *The Girl Can't Help It* (1956)
15. c) Carl Perkins
16. *Romeo and Juliet*

DECADE BY DECADE
Quiz 2: The Sixties

1. '(I Can't Get No) Satisfaction', in 1965
2. a) *Elvis Is Back!*
3. John Entwistle
4. 'You Don't Have to Say You Love Me'
5. Choose from: The Spencer Davis Group, Traffic, Blind Faith
6. c) 24
7. *Mary Poppins* (1964)
8. Otis Redding, with '(Sittin' On) The Dock of the Bay'
9. a) 'Sunshine of Your Love'
10. c) *The Wind in the Willows*, by Kenneth Grahame (1908)
11. Brian Wilson
12. The Byrds (David Crosby), Buffalo Springfield (Stephen Stills), The Hollies (Graham Nash)
13. b) 'Where Did Our Love Go', in 1964
14. Carole King
15. c) Their first three singles all reached No.1 in the UK
16. Bob Dylan

DECADE BY DECADE
Quiz 3: The Seventies

1. c) 'Smoke on the Water'
2. They simultaneously topped both the UK and US singles and albums charts
3. a) Mick Ronson
4. Van Morrison
5. The Commodores
6. Sex Pistols
7. *Catch a Fire*, by The Wailers
8. 'New Rose' (1976), by The Damned
9. a) 'Le Freak'
10. c) Country, BlueGrass and Blues
11. Curtis Mayfield
12. b) Bay City Rollers
13. b) 'Hot Love', in 1971
14. 'Hotel California', by Eagles
15. Eva Perón
16. c) 1974

DECADE BY DECADE
Quiz 4: The Eighties

1. Nirvana, 'Come as You Are'
2. c) 'Express Yourself'
3. 'Radio Ga Ga'
4. 'Relax'
5. b) *A View to a Kill* (1985)
6. Metallica
7. *Purple Rain*, by Prince and the Revolution
8. c) Tina Turner
9. Choose from: 'The Girl Is Mine', 'Billie Jean', 'Beat It', 'Wanna Be Startin' Somethin'', 'Human Nature', 'P.Y.T. (Pretty Young Thing)' and 'Thriller'
10. USA for Africa, 'We Are the World'
11. c) 'Sweet Child o' Mine', in 1988
12. c) *Fear of a Black Planet* (1989)
13. *Graceland* (1986)
14. Happy Mondays
15. b) 1986
16. *3 Feet High and Rising*, by De La Soul

DECADE BY DECADE
Quiz 5: The Nineties

1. The Verve. The album was *Urban Hymns*
2. *Doggystyle*
3. Chuck D, of Public Enemy
4. a) 1993
5. Rickie Lee Jones
6. b) *Dangerous*, by Michael Jackson
7. 'Love Is All Around'
8. Hanson
9. c) 1998
10. Pulp
11. True
12. Marilyn Manson
13. c) 'The Most Beautiful Girl in the World', in 1994
14. *Supernatural*
15. 'Never Ever', by All Saints
16. a) The Rembrandts

DECADE BY DECADE
Quiz 6: The New Millennium

1. The Killers. You'll see the name on the drum kit in the video for 'Mr Brightside'
2. a) 'Despacito' (2017), by Luis Fonsi feat. Daddy Yankee, with more than 5.8 billion views
3. The White Stripes
4. 50 Cent
5. c) Most words in a hit single – 1,560 in 6 minutes 4 seconds
6. Gareth Gates
7. c) Katy Perry. She earned $83 million in the period June 2017 to June 2018, according to Forbes
8. Franz Ferdinand
9. c) Shakira
10. a) Justin Bieber. The tracks were: 'Love Yourself' (No.1), 'Sorry' (No.2) and 'What Do You Mean?' (No.3)
11. Arctic Monkeys
12. a) Drake – from 'Best I Ever Had' on 23 May 2009 to the last weeks on the chart for 'Passionfruit' and 'Signs' on 19 August 2017
13. It was the first video to have 1 billion views
14. c) 'Rolling in the Deep', by Adele, with sales in excess of 28.8 million, as of January 2019
15. Barbra Streisand
16. b) All three singles sold 10 million copies worldwide

GENRES
Quiz 1: Lively Up Yourself

1. a) Burning Spear
2. UB40
3. Augustus Pablo
4. b) Eric Clapton
5. b) Lyceum Theatre, London
6. c) Steel Pulse
7. c) First winner of the Grammy for Best Reggae Album
8. Junior Murvin
9. Lee 'Scratch' Perry
10. Althea & Donna
11. c) Janet Kay
12. b) Toots and the Maytals
13. Dawn Penn
14. Peter Tosh
15. Blondie
16. 'Rivers of Babylon'. It was paired with the B-side 'Brown Girl in the Ring'

GENRES
Quiz 2: Never Mind the Bollocks

1. a) 'Anarchy in the UK'
2. 'Should I Stay or Should I Go'
3. Buzzcocks
4. Richard Hell
5. Dead Kennedys
6. a) 'Help!'
7. c) The Nipple Erectors, aka The Nips
8. The Slits
9. 'No More Heroes', by The Stranglers
10. *Ramones* (1976), by Ramones
11. c) New York Dolls
12. b) Nirvana
13. c) 'Connection'
14. Siouxsie and the Banshees
15. Stiff Little Fingers
16. X-Ray Spex

GENRES
Quiz 3: Burn This Disco Down

1. Barry White
2. 'Kung Fu Fighting'
3. c) 'I Will Survive', by Gloria Gaynor
4. b) Giorgio Moroder
5. *Saturday Night Fever*
6. *The New York Times*
7. b) Sister Sledge
8. a) 'Good Times', by Chic
9. Diana Ross
10. *Moulin Rouge!*
11. KC and the Sunshine Band
12. c) Kiss
13. b) 'Disco Inferno'
14. True
15. Rose Royce
16. b) Thousands of disco records were destroyed in 'Disco Demolition Night'

GENRES
Quiz 4: Rock'n'Roll Ain't Noise Pollution

1. Black Sabbath, Led Zeppelin and Deep Purple
2. b) Coldplay
3. Def Leppard
4. *Houses of the Holy* (1975)
5. c) Bruce Dickinson
6. c) Ronnie James Dio
7. c) 50 million
8. *Use Your Illusion II* reached No.1; its predecessor stalled at No.2
9. Anthrax, Megadeth, Metallica and Slayer
10. c) *Hammersmith*
11. Steven Tyler and Joe Perry of Aerosmith
12. a) Rick Rubin
13. Judas Priest
14. Linkin Park
15. Slipknot
16. Marilyn Manson

GENRES
Quiz 5: Straight Outta Compton

1. Grandmaster Flash and the Furious Five
2. 'Rapture'
3. c) *Do the Right Thing*
4. Choose from: RZA, Method Man, Ol' Dirty Bastard, Ghostface Killah, Raekwon, GZA, U-God, Inspectah Deck, Cappadonna or Masta Killa
5. b) *Licensed to Ill*
6. De La Soul
7. c) Ice Cube
8. MC Hammer
9. Lil' Kim
10. Lauryn Hill
11. Biggie Smalls (aka The Notorious B.I.G.) and Tupac Shakur (aka 2Pac)
12. Missy Elliott
13. a) Jay-Z
14. OutKast
15. *To Pimp a Butterfly*
16. Donald Trump

GENRES
Quiz 6: Cigarettes and Alcohol

1. b) Both were the fastest-selling debut album in the UK for a time
2. c) 'Some Might Say'
3. c) Sheffield
4. Supergrass
5. b) 'No More Heroes'
6. *Modern Life is Rubbish* (1993), by Blur
7. b) Pulp
8. b) Scott Walker
9. The Union Jack
10. Bernard Butler
11. c) 'A Design for Life'
12. b) William Blake
13. The Bluetones
14. The La's
15. Echobelly
16. The Boo Radleys

GENRES
Quiz 7: Eat, Sleep, Rave, Repeat

1. a) 'I Feel Love', by Donna Summer
2. Kraftwerk
3. M|A|R|R|S
4. 'Theme from S-Express', by S-Express
5. a) Derrick May
6. Orbital. They are named after the M25 motorway, which surrounds London. It was widely used during the illegal rave scene of the late 1980s and early 1990s
7. Underworld
8. Daft Punk
9. 'Smack My Bitch Up'
10. Jason Nevins
11. Goldie
12. The Chemical Brothers
13. c) Skrillex
14. c) 2005
15. Calvin Harris
16. Deadmau5

GENRES
Quiz 8: Grime Wave

1. Roll Deep
2. '21 Seconds'
3. 'P's and Q's'
4. 'Oi!'
5. Lord of the Mics
6. Dizzee Rascal in 2003, with *Boy in da Corner*; Skepta in 2016, with *Konnichiwa*
7. Stormzy, with *Gang Signs & Prayer* (2017)
8. Chip (formerly Chipmunk)
9. *Original Pirate Material* (2002)
10. 'Pow! (Forward)' (aka 'Forward Riddim')
11. Jme
12. DJ Slimzee
13. David Cameron
14. Kanye West
15. Drake
16. Wiley

CONTROVERSY
Quiz 1: Live and Dangerous

1. Ozzy Osbourne – though he later claimed that he didn't know it was real at the time. In January 2019, a toy bat with detachable head went on sale to commemorate the event. (No, really.)
2. c) He threw it into the audience, who ripped it apart
3. The Who. Keith Moon had passed out while playing drums.
4. Janet Jackson. She was singing with Justin Timberlake.
5. a) Altamont Speedway, California
6. b) Exposing himself
7. c) The band performed behind a screen
8. Kurt Cobain
9. b) 'Wonderwall'
10. c) He and his band 'went electric', using electric guitars and amplifiers for the first time
11. b) She flipped a middle finger at the camera
12. Sinéad O'Connor
13. Eminem
14. c) They were accompanied by strippers for one song
15. It included a tribute to the Black Panther movement and Malcolm X
16. b) Jimi Hendrix

CONTROVERSY
Quiz 2: Excess All Areas

1. Whitney Houston
2. b) Jerry Lee Lewis
3. Boy George
4. c) He snorted a line of ants
5. Phil Spector
6. Iggy Pop. The album was *Metallic K.O.* (1976)
7. Keith Moon
8. Izzy Stradlin
9. b) Ozzy Osbourne
10. Michael Jackson
11. The Clash
12. True
13. Billy Idol
14. Fleetwood Mac. The album was *Rumours* (1977)
15. Queen. And the album was *Jazz* (1978)
16. c) He rode a lawnmower into town

CONTROVERSY
Quiz 3: Can't Say That on the Radio

1. The BBC thought it might be offensive to stutterers
2. False. It was banned because of an original reference to 'Coca-Cola' – the BBC wouldn't play anything that smacked of product placement.
3. True. The ban was by pirate station Radio London.
4. As a 'death disc', its subject matter was deemed too mournful for public broadcast
5. b) Ronald Reagan
6. 'Creep'
7. Because of the UK's war with Argentina over the Falkland Islands
8. False. It was banned because of its supposed sexual content.
9. Several US radio stations felt that it was blasphemous
10. b) Radio stations felt that singer Jack Ely's slurred delivery was designed to hide rude words
11. c) Because they couldn't decipher his cryptic lyrics and were concerned that they might be spreading rude or politically controversial ideas
12. Margaret Thatcher. 'One of the most controversial chart contenders of all time', noted the UK's Official Charts Company.
13. a) Some listeners felt the lyrics suggested sexual harassment and hinted at date rape
14. c) The idea of an astronaut getting lost in space seemed in poor taste while the Moon mission was ongoing
15. a) 'In the Air Tonight'. Authorities believed it might remind listeners of airborne missiles
16. b) 'Friggin' in the Riggin''

CONTROVERSY
Quiz 4: Court Is in Session

1. 'Blurred Lines', by Robin Thicke
2. Foxy Brown
3. Morrissey
4. Mick Jagger and Keith Richards
5. a) 'He's So Fine', by The Chiffons
6. b) 'Shakermaker'
7. 'Surfin' USA'
8. 'Come Together'
9. 'Viva la Vida'
10. c) Judas Priest
11. Not guilty
12. Pussy Riot
13. 'Da Ya Think I'm Sexy?' (1978)
14. a) 'Father and Son'
15. c) John Mortimer

CONTROVERSY
Quiz 5: Fashion Killa

1. Lady Gaga
2. A pink cone bra and corset. The star was Madonna
3. CeeLo Green, of Gnarls Barkley
4. a) Nicki Minaj
5. b) Machine guns attached to an arm sleeve
6. A dress
7. c) They were see-through plastic – and he wasn't wearing underwear
8. Peter Gabriel
9. Dave Hill of Slade
10. A swastika
11. Prince
12. Björk
13. Brian Jones
14. Kevin Rowland
15. 'Have You Seen Your Mother, Baby, Standing in the Shadow?'
16. a) A full-body burqa

CONTROVERSY
Quiz 6: My Beautiful Dark Twisted Life

1. Take your pick from: Beck, Taylor Swift, Justice and Simian
2. b) Barack Obama (then President of the USA)
3. b) A choice
4. c) Jesus Christ
5. Taylor Swift
6. a) Martin Louis the King Jr
7. True
8. c) 'Famous'
9. c) It featured the Confederate flag
10. c) He had a 'co-star' in the form of an actor dressed as Jesus Christ
11. 'Monster'
12. Mark Zuckerberg
13. a) The 13th Amendment (which legally ended the practice of slavery in the USA). He later qualified 'abolish' to 'amend'
14. Kanye implied that he would have sex with any of his wife Kim Kardashian's four sisters
15. c) New Artist of the Year

ON RECORD
Quiz 1: Cover to Cover

1. Peter Blake and Jann Haworth
2. a) Robert Crumb
3. Roger Dean
4. Robert Mapplethorpe
5. b) Jamie Reid
6. b) *Artpop* (2013)
7. a) Radio waves from a pulsar
8. *The Holy Bible* (1994)
9. New Order, 'Blue Monday'
10. a) *The Velvet Underground and Nico* (1967), by The Velvet Underground and Nico
11. c) A corpse with a tag reading 'Uncle Sam' on its toe
12. All the sleeves feature photographs of the rappers as children
13. Edouard Manet
14. *Born in the USA* (1984)
15. a) *Licensed to Ill* (1986)

ON RECORD
Quiz 2: Wall of Sound

1. b) 'Be My Baby', by The Ronettes (1963). It stalled at No.2
2. Trevor Horn
3. a) Butch Vig
4. Amy Winehouse
5. *The Grey Album*
6. Sam Phillips
7. *Never Mind the Bollocks, Here's the Sex Pistols* (1977)
8. Daniel Lanois
9. Brian Eno
10. *OK Computer*, by Radiohead
11. Lee 'Scratch' Perry
12. Dr. Dre
13. c) Rick Rubin
14. c) Quincy Jones
15. Joe Meek
16. b) *Abbey Road* (1969)

ON RECORD
Quiz 3: Who Sampled Whom?

1. 'The Last Time', by The Rolling Stones. The version sampled on 'Bitter Sweet Symphony' is an instrumental version by The Andrew Oldham Orchestra
2. 'When the Levee Breaks' (1971)
3. 'Stronger'
4. 'Nice for What'
5. 'My Name Is'
6. *3 Feet High and Rising*
7. 'You Spin Me Round (Like a Record)', by Dead or Alive
8. 'Ma Baker'
9. 'Personal Jesus'
10. 'Funky Drummer'
11. c) Around 3,000
12. False. It samples Chic's 'Good Times' (1979)
13. 'Are "Friends" Electric?' (1979), by Tubeway Army
14. a) 'How Soon Is Now?' (1984)
15. 'U Can't Touch This'
16. b) Steely Dan. The composers were Donald Fagen and Walter Becker

ON RECORD
Quiz 4: Bringing It All Back Home

1. c) Lyrics from the band's next two albums, *Amnesiac* (2001) and *Hail to the Thief* (2003)
2. The sound of an elephant's trumpet
3. c) *Atom Heart Mother* (1970)
4. *Sgt. Pepper's Lonely Hearts Club Band* (1967), by The Beatles
5. a) The black-and-white illustrations changed to colour
6. c) It was hidden in the pre-gap before the CD started
7. Stars
8. 'Eat Me' – put the number up to a mirror and you'll see what we mean
9. a) There was a double groove on one side of the original vinyl LP, each one featuring different tracks. Whichever one the stylus landed in would play
10. It originally appeared as the last track on one side of an album
11. *In Utero* (1993)
12. a) It was nominated for a Best Female Pop Vocal Grammy
13. b) *Lazaretto* (2014)
14. The Flaming Lips. The album was *Zaireeka*
15. Only one copy was ever made

ICONIC ARTISTS
Quiz 1: Elvis Presley

1. 'It's Now or Never' (1960)
2. Colonel Tom Parker, Elvis's manager
3. a) *King Creole* (1958)
4. 'Heartbreak Hotel' (1956). His last US No.1 was 'Suspicious Minds' (1969)
5. 'Hound Dog'
6. c) *The Ed Sullivan Show*
7. a) The Beatles
8. a) *Love Me Tender*
9. a) *Elvis' Christmas Album* (1957)
10. A gold lamé suit (actually a gold-leaf tuxedo)
11. c) Taking Care of Business
12. c) The International Hotel in Las Vegas
13. c) Willie Nelson
14. a) Three
15. b) He played his last concert
16. c) Bruce Springsteen

ICONIC ARTISTS
Quiz 2: The Beatles

1. c) Eduardo Paolozzi
2. 'She Loves You' (1963)
3. b) 'Cry for a Shadow'
4. *A Hard Day's Night* (1964)
5. Longest: 'Revolution 9' (1968). Shortest: 'Her Majesty' (1969)
6. a) Rory Storm and the Hurricanes
7. George Harrison, with *Wonderwall Music* (1968)
8. c) 'Bad to Me', by Billy J. Kramer and the Dakotas
9. c) 'Don't Bother Me'
10. a) 1969
11. c) Marijuana
12. c) 73 million
13. c) *Yesterday and Today*
14. 'Hey Jude' (1968)
15. Joe Cocker (1968); Wet Wet Wet (1988); Sam & Mark (2004)
16. Billy Preston

ICONIC ARTISTS
Quiz 3: The Rolling Stones

1. Muddy Waters. The track was 'Rollin' Stone' (1950)
2. Eric Stewart – although he continued working as a roadie for the band and playing keyboards for them
3. 'The Last Time' (1965)
4. 'Miss You' (1978)
5. Buddy Holly and the Crickets
6. 'Paint It, Black'
7. c) 'Let's Spend Some Time Together'
8. a) Hyde Park
9. *Performance* (1970)
10. b) France
11. Charlie Watts
12. Faces
13. Bill Wyman
14. b) Martin Scorsese
15. *Life*
16. True

ICONIC ARTISTS
Quiz 4: Sex Pistols

1. c) Saint Martin's School of Art
2. b) 'I'm Eighteen'
3. a) David Bowie (as Ziggy Stardust and the Spiders from Mars)
4. Howard Devoto and Pete Shelley
5. Queen
6. c) 'Pretty Vacant'
7. c) Buckingham Palace
8. Virgin Records
9. b) 'The First Cut Is the Deepest'/'I Don't Want to Talk About It'
10. b) Christmas Day
11. c) San Francisco
12. The Chelsea Hotel
13. Glen Matlock
14. *The Great Rock'n'Roll Swindle*
15. a/3; b/1; c/2
16. b) 1996

ICONIC ARTISTS
Quiz 5: Madonna

1. b) The Breakfast Club
2. a) Drummer
3. 'Like a Virgin' (1984)
4. Rosanna Arquette
5. Marilyn Monroe
6. c) Beastie Boys
7. *True Blue* (1986), with sales of more than 20 million
8. 'Like a Prayer'
9. Breathless Mahoney
10. *Evita* (1996)
11. b) Lenny Kravitz
12. b) 'Frozen'
13. *Austin Powers: The Spy Who Shagged Me* (1999)
14. Christina Aguilera and Britney Spears
15. c) Sticky & Sweet Tour. Staged in 2008–9, it grossed more than $407.7 million
16. False

ICONIC ARTISTS
Quiz 6: Prince

1. c) *For You* (1977)
2. *The Black Album*
3. The Revolution
4. 3RDEYEGIRL
5. 'When Doves Cry' (1984)
6. Camille
7. *Sign o' the Times* (1987)
8. Paisley Park
9. The Vault
10. The O2 Arena
11. 'While My Guitar Gently Weeps'
12. *Under the Cherry Moon* (1986)
13. b) Purple
14. 'Kiss'
15. Jehovah's Witnesses
16. He had the No.1 US single ('When Doves Cry'), box-office movie (*Purple Rain*) and album (the *Purple Rain* soundtrack)

ICONIC ARTISTS
Quiz 7: Nirvana

1. Chad Channing
2. c) CBS
3. False. They never had a *Billboard* Hot 100 No.1
4. 'About a Girl'
5. Cello
6. *In Utero* (1993)
7. b) Shocking Blue
8. Choose from: 'Come As You Are', 'Lithium' or 'In Bloom'
9. 'Endless, Nameless'
10. Accordion or organ
11. Choose from: David Bowie, Lead Belly (Huddie Ledbetter), The Vaselines or Meat Puppets
12. 'Rape Me'
13. c) A deodorant
14. b) 1992
15. c) 75 million
16. 'This Is a Call'

ICONIC ARTISTS
Quiz 8: Beyoncé

1. Giselle
2. 'Independent Women (Part 1)' (2000)
3. *Dangerously in Love* (2003)
4. True, as certified by the Recording Industry Association of America (RIAA)
5. *Lemonade* (2016)
6. 'Crazy in Love'
7. c) Foxxy Cleopatra
8. It's Beyoncé's birthday
9. The Supremes
10. Sasha Fierce
11. 'Single Ladies (Put a Ring on It)'
12. a) House of Deréon
13. 'Hold Up' (2016)
14. Lady Gaga
15. c) Tidal
16. Jay-Z

DON'T FEAR THE REAPER
Quiz 1: I'll Never Get Out of This World Alive

1. Sam Cooke
2. Otis Redding
3. Brian Jones
4. b) *L.A. Woman*
5. Gram Parsons
6. Mini
7. Keith Moon
8. Bon Scott (of AC/DC)
9. Ozzy Osbourne
10. Peter Tosh
11. Kurt Cobain
12. Tupac Shakur (1996); Biggie Smalls (aka The Notorious B.I.G.; 1997)
13. Jeff Buckley
14. Michael Hutchence
15. TLC
16. a) Jam Master Jay (of Run-DMC)

DON'T FEAR THE REAPER
Quiz 2: Someone Saved My Life Tonight

1. Choose from: Buddy Holly, Ritchie Valens or 'The Big Bopper' (aka Jiles Perry 'J.P.' Richardson Jr)
2. Dave Gahan, of Depeche Mode
3. a) Nikki Sixx
4. Jerry Lee Lewis
5. Keith Richards
6. b) Izzy Stradlin
7. John Lydon
8. Ozzy Osbourne
9. Josh Homme
10. c) Duff McKagan
11. 50 Cent
12. Eminem
13. Elton John
14. Donna Summer

DON'T FEAR THE REAPER
Quiz 3: Dead Man's Curve

1.   c) Jerry Leiber and Mike Stoller
2.   c) Her boyfriend's class ring
3.   c) They drown
4.   He crashed in a stock-car race
5.   'Johnny Remember Me'
6.   'I Don't Like Mondays', by The Boomtown Rats
7.   c) George 'Shadow' Morton
8.   'Terry'
9.   'Dead Man's Curve'
10.   Bobbie Gentry
11.   'Seasons in the Sun', by Terry Jacks
12.   'Emma'
13.   'Detroit Rock City'
14.   'Hello, This Is Joannie (The Telephone Answering Machine Song)'
15.   'Sometimes It Snows in April'
16.   'Stan' (2000)

DON'T FEAR THE REAPER
Quiz 4: Last Rites

1. Both were gravediggers
2. Marc Almond
3. c) He was shot
4. Ian Dury
5. Paul McCartney
6. Dave Grohl
7. b) Michael Jackson
8. Marc Bolan
9. The Pretenders
10. a) Tupac Shakur
11. b) 'Three Steps to Heaven'
12. David Bowie
13. c) The head of Selena's fan club
14. Def Leppard
15. a) 'I'll Never Get Out of This World Alive'
16. c) Sid Vicious (he was just 21)

MOVING PICTURES
Quiz 1: I Hear a New World

1. *Pulp Fiction* (1994)
2. *American Graffiti*
3. The Doors
4. Simon and Garfunkel
5. Jonny Greenwood
6. *O Brother, Where Art Thou?*
7. c) *The Bodyguard* (1992), with 17 million copies plus sold
8. Pop Will Eat Itself
9. a) *Blackboard Jungle* (1955)
10. Jimmy Cliff
11. Kendrick Lamar
12. Daft Punk
13. *He Got Game*
14. *Juice*
15. *The Life Aquatic with Steve Zissou* (2004)
16. a) *Snow White and the Seven Dwarfs*. The movie came out in 1937; the soundtrack was released in 1938

MOVING PICTURES
Quiz 2: Video Killed the Radio Star

1. 'Big Time Sensuality'
2. 'The Rain (Supa Dupa Fly)'
3. 'Sledgehammer', by Peter Gabriel
4. 'Sabotage'
5. 'Humble'
6. 'Hey Ya!'
7. 'Take On Me', by A-ha
8. b) *8½*
9. Spike Jonze
10. b) He isn't in it
11. 'Notorious'
12. Anton Corbijn
13. 'Look What You Made Me Do'
14. c) Gus Van Sant
15. a) $500,000
16. Morphing

MOVING PICTURES
Quiz 3: If You Will, Rockumentary

1. Backing singers
2. The Originals
3. Blur
4. The Maysles Brothers
5. *Dig!*
6. Sex Pistols
7. Metallica
8. 'Subterranean Homesick Blues'
9. *Scratch*
10. Sixto Rodriguez
11. Jimmy Page, The Edge and Jack White
12. *Meeting People Is Easy*
13. D.A. Pennebaker
14. Chet Baker
15. Some audience members were given digital cameras with which they recorded a Beasties gig at Madison Square Garden
16. c) George Harrison

MOVING PICTURES
Quiz 4: Everyone's Gone to the Movies

1. Justin Timberlake
2. Choose from Judy Garland, Barbra Streisand or Lady Gaga. The original movie version in 1937 starred Janet Gaynor, but she played the part of an actress, not a singer
3. *Two-Lane Blacktop* (1971)
4. Ice-T
5. c) *Rise of the Planet of the Apes*
6. *King Creole* (1958)
7. *Pat Garrett and Billy the Kid*
8. a/3; b/1; c/2
9. b) Frank Sinatra
10. *Boyz n the Hood* (1991)
11. Tom Waits
12. Jennifer Lopez
13. Will Smith
14. Janet Jackson
15. *Hidden Figures*
16. Courtney Love

FORMED A BAND
Quiz 1: The Singer Not the Song

1. The Rolling Stones
2. Ludacris
3. Kylie Minogue
4. Terry Reid
5. Duran Duran
6. Paul Di'Anno
7. Nusrat Fateh Ali Khan
8. a) Whitney Houston
9. c) Ariana Grande. In February 2019, 'Break Up with Your Girlfriend, I'm Bored' replaced '7 Rings' as the UK's No.1 single
10. Frank Sinatra
11. 'Low'
12. c) Elvis Presley
13. b) Dr. Dre
14. *Boy in da Corner* (2003)
15. a) Britney Spears
16. c) Drake

FORMED A BAND
Quiz 2: Careful with That Axe, Eugene

1. Jeff Beck
2. Jack White
3. Girlschool
4. a) Finsbury Park Astoria, London
5. He lost two of his fingertips in an industrial accident
6. John McLaughlin
7. Dave Mustaine
8. John Frusciante
9. b) Gene Vincent
10. Bo Diddley
11. Johnny Marr; The Smiths
12. John Squire
13. Slash
14. T-Bone Walker
15. Prince
16. Scotty Moore

FORMED A BAND
Quiz 3: The Low End Theory

1. Flea
2. Carol Kaye
3. Bootsy Collins
4. b) James Jamerson
5. Gail Ann Dorsey
6. Cliff Williams
7. Melissa Auf der Maur
8. Captain Sensible
9. c) It had 12 strings
10. a) Rickenbacker
11. b) Herbie Flowers
12. a) Fender. The Fender Precision Bass appeared in 1951
13. c) Bill Wyman, in 1961
14. Kim Deal
15. a) Larry Graham
16. Thundercat

FORMED A BAND
Quiz 4: We Got the Beat

1. Tommy Lee, of Mötley Crüe
2. c) 'Funky Drummer'
3. a) Two bass drums
4. Ginger Baker; Cream
5. Hal Blaine
6. Tony Allen
7. b) Carlton Barrett
8. Jaki Liebezeit; Can
9. Oasis
10. Sheila E.
11. Stevie Wonder
12. c) Carl Palmer
13. Chic
14. John Bonham, of Led Zeppelin
15. Cozy Powell
16. The Velvet Underground

FORMED A BAND
Quiz 5: Big Boss Man

1. Don Arden. The act was Small Faces
2. Sharon Osbourne. Her husband is Ozzy
3. c) X-Ray Spex
4. Peter Grant. The band in question was Led Zeppelin
5. David Bowie
6. Terence Stamp
7. Albert Grossman
8. a) Backstreet Boys
9. c) Bee Gees
10. Beyoncé. Mathew Knowles is her father
11. Jon Landau
12. Simon Fuller
13. U2
14. c) Scooter Braun
15. Celine Dion
16. Svengali

FORMED A BAND
Quiz 6: We Are Family

1. Robert Smith. He played with all three of them in the 1980s
2. Boy George
3. The Teardrop Explodes (Julian Cope); Echo and the Bunnymen (Ian McCulloch); Wah!, The Mighty Wah!, Wah Heat!, Say Wah! Pete Wylie and the Oedipus Wrecks (the most successful variants of bands fronted by Pete Wylie)
4. John Mayall & the Bluesbreakers
5. Choose from: Free (Paul Rodgers and Simon Kirke), Mott the Hoople (Mick Ralphs) or King Crimson (Boz Burrell)
6. The band was The Move. The musicians were Roy Wood, Bev Bevan and Jeff Lynne
7. Bobby Gillespie
8. Craig Gannon
9. Flea; Duff McKagan
10. Rod Stewart and Ronnie Wood
11. Tom Tom Club
12. New Order. They comprise Stephen Morris and Gillian Gilbert
13. Choose from Beats International, Freak Power, Pizzaman or Mighty Dub Katz
14. Nick Cave
15. Andy Bell
16. Fun Boy Three

FESTIVALS
Quiz 1: Were You There?

1. a) Big Brother and the Holding Company (featuring Janis Joplin)
2. Otis Redding
3. He had been shot in a failed assassination attempt just two days before
4. Isle of Wight
5. Jimi Hendrix
6. c) Rage Against the Machine
7. Prince
8. Lady Gaga
9. c) The crowd finished off the set by singing the rest of the song
10. b) David Bowie finishing his 2000 set with an encore of '"Heroes"'
11. Coachella
12. Dolly Parton
13. Woodstock '94
14. c) Peanut butter
15. A blue tank, which played techno. It was later bought by Don Henley of the Eagles
16. a) In a giant glass 'hamster' ball

FESTIVALS
Quiz 2: Three Days of Peace & Music

1. False. To name just one larger gathering, Donauinselfest – held on an island in Vienna's River Danube – pulls in around 3 million visitors every year
2. a) Creedence Clearwater Revival
3. b) Richie Havens
4. Jimi Hendrix. He was backed by his band Gypsy Sun and Rainbows
5. c) He threw it into the audience
6. Santana. The song is 'Soul Sacrifice'
7. Sha Na Na
8. Janis Joplin
9. The Lovin' Spoonful
10. Country Joe McDonald
11. c) The Doors. They were asked but turned down the chance to appear
12. b) Water buffaloes in India
13. 'Purple Haze', by Jimi Hendrix with Gypsy Sun and Rainbows
14. Joni Mitchell. Her boyfriend, Graham Nash, did play at Woodstock, with his band Crosby, Stills, Nash & Young
15. b) Martin Scorsese
16. c) Around $1.4 million

FESTIVALS
Quiz 3: Going Up the Country

1. £1 – including free milk
2. T. Rex
3. Pulp
4. Robbie Williams
5. Arctic Monkeys
6. Kanye West
7. a) Nothing – it's free to them
8. b) 1981
9. John Williams
10. b) She wore a bullet-proof vest
11. Billy Bragg
12. A single white glove
13. Matt Smith
14. Beyoncé
15. Florence + the Machine
16. The Dalai Lama

FESTIVALS
Quiz 4: Closing Acts

1. c) 50 Cent
2. a) Perry Farrell of Jane's Addiction
3. Woodstock from Peanuts (first named in print on 22 June 1970), created by Charles M. Schulz
4. All the acts were solo female artists or female-led bands
5. Desert Trip
6. True. The Lower Keys Underwater Music Festival takes place annually in Florida, USA
7. Austin, Texas, USA
8. Latitude
9. Burning Man
10. a) 1 second
11. *The Prisoner*
12. Radiohead
13. Bill Graham
14. Monsters of Rock
15. Peter Gabriel
16. Because of its connections with the novel *Dracula* (1897), by Bram Stoker. In the story, Count Dracula comes ashore in England at Whitby

THANK YOU AND GOODNIGHT
Quiz 1: On This Day in History

1. Marvin Gaye, *What's Going On*
2. Live Aid
3. 'Fuck tha Police', by N.W.A.
4. b) He was drafted into the US Army
5. Blur, 'Country House'; Oasis, 'Roll with It'
6. He changed his name to an unpronounceable symbol
7. Eric Carr, of Kiss
8. Metallica
9. a) Rihanna
10. Most simultaneous singles in the US Top 10. He had seven
11. 'Viva la Vida'
12. *Pop Idol*
13. Tamla (Motown)
14. 'Waterloo'
15. On the rooftop of the Apple Corps headquarters
    (at 3 Savile Row, London)
16. The Concert for New York City

THANK YOU AND GOODNIGHT
Quiz 2: The First Cut Is the Deepest

1. Justin Bieber and Katy Perry
2. DJ Jazzy Jeff and the Fresh Prince (for 'Parents Just Don't Understand', in 1989)
3. It was the first million-selling record
4. It was the first album to sell one million copies in a week
5. c) Spice Girls
6. Taylor Swift, for *Fearless* (2010) and *1989* (2014)
7. 'Video Killed the Radio Star' (1981), by Buggles
8. The Beatles' concert at Shea Stadium on 15 August 1965
9. *The Visitors* (1982), by ABBA
10. *Bad* (1987), by Michael Jackson
11. Ed Sheeran (in 2017, with 'Shape of You' [No.1] and 'Castle on the Hill' [No.6])
12. It won Grammys for Song of the Year and Record of the Year, the first hip hop track to claim either. It also picked up Grammys for Best Music Video and Best Rap/Sung Collaboration
13. 'Je t'aime ... moi non plus' (1969), by Serge Gainsbourg and Jane Birkin
14. 'The Masses Against the Classes', by Manic Street Preachers. It took the top spot from Westlife on 16 January 2000
15. c) Beyoncé, in 2003. Rihanna and Ariana Grande subsequently achieved the same feat
16. *Licensed to Ill* (1987), by Beastie Boys

THANK YOU AND GOODNIGHT
Quiz 3: Some Might Say

1. Lou Reed (*Uncut*, 2003)
2. Lemmy (in an interview on *The Old Grey Whistle Test*)
3. b) Donald Trump (*The Guardian*, 2017)
4. Freddie Mercury (*The Daily Mail*, 1978)
5. Kanye West
6. Prince
7. Madonna
8. b) Rihanna (*Rolling Stone*, 2013)
9. Noel Gallagher, talking about Blur (*NME*, 1995)
10. Tom Waits (*NME*, 1983)
11. c) John Lydon on Sid Vicious (*NME*, 1978)
12. a) Héloïse Letissier (Christine of Christine and the Queens)
13. a) Lady Gaga (*Rolling Stone*, 2010)
14. c) Debbie Harry (*The Sunday Times Magazine*, 2017)
15. Kate Bush (*MOJO*, 2015)

THANK YOU AND GOODNIGHT
Quiz 4: I Know Where Syd Barrett Lives

1. J Dilla
2. Laurie Anderson
3. Yoko Ono
4. Scott Walker
5. The BBC Radiophonic Workshop
6. Sun Ra. He claimed to be from Saturn
7. Mark Hollis
8. Bill Drummond
9. *Good Will Hunting*
10. Nick Drake
11. 'See Emily Play'. It got to No.6 in 1967
12. Peaches
13. Lee Mavers
14. Aphex Twin
15. Alex Chilton
16. Elizabeth 'Liz' Fraser

THANK YOU AND GOODNIGHT
Quiz 5: This Is My Truth Tell Me Yours

1. False. She died from heart failure.
2. True. Their blood was added to the red ink.
3. True – it was a double bed shaped like a coffin.
4. True. Beach Boy Dennis Wilson's song 'Never Learn Not to Love' was an adaptation of Manson's 'Cease to Exist' and became the B-side of a 1968 single by the group, 'Bluebirds Over the Mountain'. Manson received a cash payment and motorcycle for the song.
5. False. The story was first reported by John Lennon, but Paul McCartney later scotched it, explaining that the Fabs had nipped out for a (non-jazz) cigarette to calm their nerves prior to the ceremony.
6. False. Although he did once accidentally back a car into a pond.
7. True. It's named 'Callin' Oates'.
8. False
9. False. It was reportedly the name of a band that appeared in a dream to Jonathan King, owner of UK Records (to whom the group was signed)
10. True. Aerosmith had an assistant who raised concerns about the pilots or the condition of the plane – reports vary – so the band passed.
11. False. Despite a doctor's warning, she carried on snorting cocaine until she was able to wean herself off the drug.
12. False. Apparently, Bundy never came to New York City, where Harry was living during the Seventies.
13. True. The lady was Adriana Smith; the track was 'Rocket Queen' on the band's debut *Appetite for Destruction* (1987).
14. False. Jack spread the story early on in their career, but they were actually married for a while. Unconventionally, he took her surname.
15. True. But this was no ego-driven rock-star frivolity. Van Halen inserted the clause in their contract to check whether the promoter had actually read it. The band figured (correctly) that if promoters ignored this detail, they might also gloss over some of the safety requirements and checks – a genuine concern, as Van Halen were touring with massive and complex lighting equipment and stage sets at the time .
16. True. The album is *Don Juan's Reckless Daughter* (1977).

THANK YOU AND GOODNIGHT
Quiz 6: Living with the NME

1. Julie Burchill and Tony Parsons
2. Nick Kent
3. 11
4. b) 1965
5. Elvis Presley and John Peel
6. a) 307,000 plus. The actual figure was 307,217, as reported in February 2016
7. b) Top 12
8. *The Stone Roses*, by The Stone Roses
9. a) T. Rex and Oasis
10. Kraftwerk
11. They each received a 10/10 review
12. Noel Gallagher and Oasis's *Definitely Maybe*
13. It was the last printed *NME*
14. Steve Lamacq
15. Public Enemy
16. c) 'Smells Like Teen Spirit', by Nirvana

LAURENCE KING

Published in 2019 by
Laurence King Publishing Ltd
361–373 City Road
London EC1V 1LR
United Kingdom
email: enquiries@laurenceking.com
www.laurenceking.com

By arrangement with New Music Limited
NME logo © New Music Limited 2019
Text © 2019 Laurence King Publishing Ltd
Illustrations © 2019 Stéphane Manel

A catalogue record for this book
is available from the British Library

ISBN: 978-1-78627-529-5

Senior Editor: Felicity Maunder
Design: Florian Michelet
Illustrations: Stéphane Manel

Printed in Italy

Laurence King Publishing is committed to
ethical and sustainable production. We are
proud participants in The Book Chain Project
Bookchainproject.com ®